From the Inspire Ca

GW00468190

What if...

YOUR WORK AND
INTERESTS
WERE IN HARMONY?

Special free bonus gifts for you

To help you achieve more success, there are free bonus
resources for you at:

www.FreeGiftsFromDavid.com

- Three training videos on how to make
  your next career transition

- Downloadable audio training called
  "fitting into the world of work today"

David Carey

Msc, DMS, PGDip, C.Eng, MIET, MCMI

Published by 4thoughts for David Carey Inspire Career Consultancy

Disclaimer and/or legal notices

While all attempts have been made to verify information provided in this book and its ancillary materials, neither the author or publisher assumes any responsibility for errors, inaccuracies or omissions and is not responsible for any financial loss by any customer in any manner. Any slights of people or organisations are unintentional. If advice concerning legal, financial, accounting or related matters is needed, the services of a qualified professional should be sought. This book and its associated ancillary materials, including verbal and written training, is not intended for use as a source of legal, financial or accounting advice. You should be aware of the various laws governing business transactions or other business practices in your particular geographical location.

Earnings and income disclaimer

With respect to the reliability, accuracy, timeliness, usefulness, adequacy, completeness, and or suitability of information provided in this book David Carey, and Inspire Career Consultancy, 4thoughts Publishing, Partners, Associates, Affiliates, Consultants and all presenters make no warranties, guarantees, representations, or claims of any kind. Readers results will vary depending on a number of factors. Any and all claims or representation as to income earnings are not to be considered as average earnings. Testimonials are not representative. This book and all products and services are for education and informational purposes only. Use caution and see the advice of qualified professionals. Check with your accountant, attorney or professional advisor before acting on this or any information. You agree that David Carey and/or David Carey of Inspire Career Consultancy and or 4thoughts Publishing is not responsible for the success or failure of your personal, business, health or financial decisions relating to any information presented by David Carey, Inspire Career Consultancy, or company products/ services. Earnings potential is entirely dependent on the efforts, skills and application of the individual person.

Any examples, stories, references, or case studies are for illustrative purposes only and should not be interpreted as testimonies and/or examples of what reader and/or consumers can generally expect from the information. No representation in any part of this information, materials and/or seminar training are guarantees or promises for actual performance. Any statements, strategies, concepts, techniques, exercises and ideas in the information, materials and/or seminar training offered are simply opinion or experience, and thus should not be misinterpreted as promises, typical results or guarantees (expressed or implied). The author and publisher David Carey, Inspire Career Consultancy or any of David Carey's representatives shall in no way, and in any circumstances, be held liable to any party (or third-party) for any direct, indirect, punitive, special, incidental or other consequential damages arising directly or indirectly from any use of books, materials and/or seminar trainings which is provided "as is" and without warranties.

All pictures are from **Pexels.com** or drawn and copyright by Laura Carey (Shown by LC on drawings).

Printed in the United Kingdom and separately by Amazon KDP worldwide

Issue 1 December 2022 ISBN 9781906654085

WHAT OTHERS ARE SAYING ABOUT DAVID AND INSPIRE CAREER CONSULTANCY

"In May 2004, after working for Royal Mail for over 40 years, I found that my professional life seemed to be over. I took voluntary redundancy and was put into contact with your company. Feeling that I still had a lot to give put me at an all-time personal low – then I was contacted by David Carey who provided the enthusiasm, drive and insight to get me off the floor and point me in the right direction. I just cannot say how much he has helped me."

Mike J Matti, Royal Mail (ex HR Manager)

"I feel I've had the best service possible; David has not only been constructively helpful – and very much so – but his manner made him a pleasure to deal with; he is so professional. I can say with confidence that I feel prepared to face the outside world."

Sheila Wardell, Royal Mail

"David possessed a genuine desire to help me. He made me feel as though my worries and concerns about my career, and the way my life was going, were all important and more significantly that he could help me find a way out of my problems."

Elizabeth Sawyer (ex-teacher)

"David helped reignite my passion for going to work he helped me to realise the tools I had already and the things I needed to grow and what I needed to achieve to reach my ultimate goal. Working with David it took two sessions to realise what my dream job was. David was brilliant and the tools he uses on you are really brilliant and easy to use. The future looks really bright for me thanks to David."

Oliver Simpson (housing manager)

"I am writing to say that our delegate on the active retirement course was delighted with it and found it to be very interesting and informative. She found David to be a very warm, caring and enthusiastic man who genuinely wants people to get the most out of their retirement."

Stuart Burton, managing director, Paul partitioning Ltd

"I would just like to pass my thanks to you for the workshop you delivered on "starting your career - the key questions". Myself and my students found it very worthwhile."

Jed Brazier Assistant- Director Bournemouth Business School International

"You helped me to focus and pull out lots of relevant ideas on which I can now rebuild a plan to the future. It is a daunting prospect to be embarking on something completely new and different to what I had done before, but with your support and advice I now feel well prepared and raring to go."

Lara Melhuish

"I found out about Inspire Career Consultancy through the Yellow Pages and it was a moment of great despair I must say and I was really looking for help. Inspire helped me by uncovering something I had almost lost and that was the deep value to me of my musicianship and the importance of placing music at the centre of my professional life. David is an incredible listener and he's incredibly resourceful. In many ways David has helped me to reconnect to my past and with my identity. The future looks much brighter. Nothing is quite settled yet however I feel confident that I can move into the future and give what I have to give to the world without fear or hesitation."

Fabian Lochner (special needs teacher)

"I worked with David when I was going through problems with my employment. After a few sessions with David I found that the path I was following was the right one however I needed to change my way of working which David helped me with. David also helped me produce a photographic workshop programme from start to finish which I wouldn't have been able to do on my own. He helped me with my fears of public speaking and my communication skills. He is always very thorough and knowledgeable in everything he is involved in."

Andy Whale (Photographer)

"I have changed career completely with the help of Inspire from a head teacher to an electrician. Inspire helped me by going through a number of processes which actually identified the skills and talents that I have. I found I thoroughly enjoyed the process of working out exactly what I would be doing and where I would be going. David tailors what he is going to do to you. You are really getting individual help and individual care about where your life is going and where you are going next."

Ben Howden (primary school Head Teacher)

"Under David's professional guidance and support, I dedicated time to really analyse myself from both a personal and commercial viewpoint. This was both a challenge and a big awakening for me.

The toolkits David provided coupled with regular two-way discussions, idea generation and defined action plans, culminated in me starting to understand what my own values were, my skill set and ultimately, what made me happy and rewarded.

At such a critical stage in my life where my decisions were going to impact the rest of my working life, I now had the confidence and understanding to formalise an alternative career path. I can honestly say that without David's tutelage, I would not have gifted myself the time or dedication to reach this stage of my personal career journey."

Lisa Caveny—Barton

MOTIVATE AND INSPIRE OTHERS!

"Share This Book"

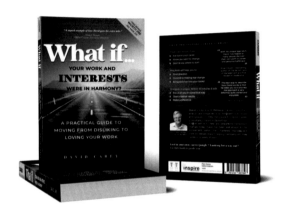

Retail	$18. 99	£12. 95
	(Amazon)	(Direct)

5 – 20 Books	£ 11. 95
21 – 99 Books	£ 9. 95
100 – 499 Books	£ 8. 95
500 – 999 Books	£ 7. 95
1000 + Books	£ 5. 95

David Carey
www.inspirecc.com/books
01202 605102
from abroad +44 1202 605102

THE IDEAL PROFESSIONAL SPEAKER FOR YOUR NEXT EVENT!

Any organisation that wants their people
to become "extraordinary" needs to hire David
for a keynote and/or workshop training!

To contact or book David to speak:

David Carey
www.inspirecc.com/speaker
01202 605102
from abroad +44 1202 605102

THE IDEAL CAREER COACH FOR YOU!

If you're ready to overcome challenges, have major breakthroughs and achieve higher levels then you will love having David as your coach!

To contact or book David :

David Carey
www.inspirecc.com/coach
01202 605102
from abroad +44 1202 605102

DEDICATION

I would like to dedicate this book to the following people:

My Mum and Dad who provided me with the education to follow my dreams.

My lovely wife Cath and children Laura and Paul who have encouraged me right from the start.

My brother Eric and my good friend Paul Moss (centre) who I sadly lost in 2021.

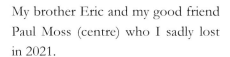

My friend Paul Booker. Paul, thank you for helping me achieve my goals over the past 15 years. I look forward to the goals yet to be achieved.

A MESSAGE FOR YOU

Thank you for buying this book.

Some of you may remember me from my days with the Chartered Management Institute, the Princes Trust, DORMEN or within corporate life. It was a great privilege to help you in those days and it is my desire to continue to do so within Inspire Career Consultancy and these books.

There are some key steps that I have learnt that have helped me successfully change my career and I want to pass them on in this book in case they can help you.

My approach will be to work with you in the same way as if you were at one of my workshops or we were working together one to one (don't worry we will be taking plenty of breaks!).

In this book we will be focusing on your interests and the part they have to play within your career.

Interests can point to the ideal field of work for you but not necessarily the job which we will be exploring later.

We will be looking at a number of tools to help you explore your current interests and maybe find some that you didn't realise you had.

After doing this we will be visiting a particular approach by a person called John Holland (his RIASEC model) which has been used worldwide to help match people's interests to their careers.

It will all come together with exploring what you have learnt on the journey and how you can use it moving forward.

I'm really excited to be joining you within these pages and making a difference to your career.

As we work together, you will be following the footsteps of many. It would be really nice to hear of your success if you would like to contact me.

As I reach this particular stage in my own career it is my heart's desire for these books to end up in the hands of people who could really benefit from them. I feel this is my mission at this time—to get alongside people on their career journeys.

With that in mind, I intend to give a lot away to good causes. Your contribution in buying this book will allow me to do this.

David Carey

davidc@inspirecc.com

www.inspirecc.com

01202 605102 from within the UK

+44 1202 605102 from abroad

Jungle

Exploring

Discovery

Committing

Future

How this book works:

- Let me start with a promise. Within 15 minutes we will be working on your career.

- I will be your guide in this personal and fun interactive journey through your own 'career jungle'.

- There are a number of engaging and thought provoking exercises to complete.

- You will end up with a valuable record of your journey, which can be reviewed at different stages within your career, to help you make key decisions.

- From time to time you will find 'recap and look forward' boxes to keep you on track and jungle maps so you don't lose your way.

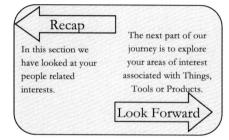

← **Recap**

In this section we have looked at your people related interests.

The next part of our journey is to explore your areas of interest associated with Things, Tools or Products.

Look Forward →

- Our time together starts by introducing you to the career jungle. This separates our journey from any other career materials you may have used.

- We start with a cup of tea, or coffee. Whenever you see the coffee cup it is your invitation to look deeper within the picture, distance yourself from the distractions of the day and really think about your situation and how you can make some changes. I am getting ahead of myself though!

Time to get that cup of coffee and I look forward to you joining me on page one and making the journey come alive.

Jungle

Exploring

DISCOVERY

COMMITTING

FUTURE

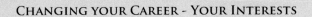

INTRODUCTION

Getting into the right mindset

WAKING FROM A DEEP SLEEP

Imagine that last night you fell asleep unsure of your future.

You felt lost, without a sense of direction.

Today, as you start to wake from a deep sleep you notice the sunrise welcoming another day.

Something is different.

As you lie there, you notice a painting of a jungle on the opposite wall.

Hazily you get drawn into it.

As the sunlight falls onto the painting you start to enter a dreamlike state.

The jungle takes form, and in the distance you can see the sunrise over the horizon and the promise of adventure ahead.

You see yourself at the start of a journey and wonder what if?

As you lie there between the world of being awake and being asleep, you find yourself floating above the jungle and realise that it is calling to you.

Looking down you see a number of paths to the horizon; some clear, some hidden and mysterious.

Considering the start of a journey.

The promise of a solution to feeling lost beckons.

Floating above the jungle — calling you to explore.

Still within this twilight zone, you are aware of the world around you.

At the same time you're still aware of the dream.

You have the power to decide what are you going to do next?

Will you wake fully and explore the jungle, or continue your life as it was the day before?

Time to decide.

Will you take some action? Will you join others who have explored the jungle before you?

If you decide to explore the jungle with me, the following is what we will achieve together.

3

WHAT WILL YOU ACHIEVE BY READING THIS BOOK?

At the end of the book, we will be celebrating that you will have achieved the following:

1. Gained an understanding of your interests by exploring:

- Your background—how you have got to where you are today
- Interests associated with your learning to date
- Interests associated with people's problems or needs
- Interests associated with things, tools or products
- Where you might fit into a typical business
- A respected tool known as the RIASEC or Holland tool

2. Generated a few possible careers using the above.

Achieving your goals.

3. Committed to some actions which will help you move forward.

The jungle is fading now. You have taken the first step to changing your career by getting this book.

Will you start the day by deciding to take your next step?

Will you let me be your guide?

Will you turn the page?

Recap

In this section you have been introduced to your journey and left with a decision, turn the page or put the book away?

After a welcome, the next part of our journey is to carry out some preliminary exercises and capture some basic career information to allow us to make a solid start on our journey together.

Look Forward

Will you take the next step?

Packing for the journey.

Welcome to your journey

Just like any other journey, there are a few things to pack before we set off. There are two things, in particular that would help us.

Aha! moments

The first is a notebook, journal, or an app where you can jot down any thoughts which pop into your head (aha! moments). You might be starting a lifelong habit here so why not treat yourself to a nice one?

An aha! journal.

What are aha! 'moments' I hear you say?

These are the moments when you realise something about yourself. It is where we start to move from 'exploration' to 'discovery'. The exercises in this book will almost certainly generate some of these.

Examples might be, aha! This is why I ...

- Loved my job at X
- Couldn't concentrate in college on Y
- Didn't fit in with my colleagues at Z

These are really precious moments.

Look out for anything which triggers an aha! moment. On your journey through this book, an aha! moment might be generated in the middle of the night. If it does, please remember to record and capture it when you wake.

When you have completed all of the exercises in the book, please refer to any aha! moments you have captured in your notebook and transfer the most important of them to exercise nine page 208.

The second thing I would suggest you pack is a review of how you've got to where you are now.

This is where we are going next as you turn the page.

Off we go!

Warm up exercise to get you started.

Preliminary exercises to get you started.

To help you review your career to date, and capture any career ideas you may have had in the past, there are a series of preliminary exercises in appendix three (page 187). These will refresh your memory providing stimulus for new, future ideas.

You may even decide to reconsider some of them.

The preliminary exercises (one to six) can be found in appendix three pages 187-205.

Getting ready for the journey.

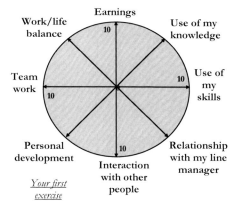

Your first exercise

Why have they been put there and not here? This is a style that has been adopted in all of the Inspire career library books to allow all of the key exercises to be collected in one place.

That way, they will be easy to find for future reference and can be viewed together.

So ... please turn to appendix three page 187 and, with a cup of tea or coffee (or maybe something stronger), tell me a little bit about yourself in exercises one to six.

Telling your story.

Please remember to capture any aha! moments in your notebook/journal.

Afterwards, return here and we will explore 'Eureka Moments'. These are particularly strong aha! moments; you may even have had some during the preliminary exercises! See you when you return from page 187.

What to do if you suddenly notice your ideal career on our journey?

WHAT TO DO IF YOU HAVE A 'EUREKA MOMENT'?

Have you ever had a 'Eureka' moment? Think of it like an extreme aha moment where something occurs to you that affects you at a very deep level that you will almost certainly action. Can you remember what it felt like? Maybe, you have already had one of these in the preliminary exercises.

Eureka

- The pieces suddenly fell into place.

- It was a perfect fit.

- It seemed obvious.

- NOW I know what I want to do!

Watch out for the Eureka moment which can change your life

Make the best use of your Eureka moment.

Many people on this journey experience such a moment. What should you do if you have one?

People nearly always report wanting to stop everything and get on with it right now. They lose interest in doing anything else. Even reading this book would be difficult.

If this is you, turn to pages 145-147 ('What to do when you have decided on your next career move and the Eureka Landing page') to find some immediate suggestions to help, and return here afterwards.

Even if you have had a Eureka moment, and you are really certain of it, you will still gain much by reading the rest of the book and after that go to page 155 ('preparing to commit to change').

On the next page we meet Kevin where we see the importance of his 'Eureka moment' and the impact on his life. After meeting Kevin, our next port of call is to look at exactly what your own interests are.

Kevin was approaching the end of a 27 year career in radio and was very fearful that he didn't have any other useable skills to take into his future.

On reading an early draft of this book Kevin came across a photo, shown below, which provided him with his own 'Eureka' moment.

The photo immediately triggered in his mind a 'Tour Guide'.

Listening to Kevin's story.

He had always loved 'playing the tour guide' to friends and family and realised that exploring a career as a 'tour guide' was exciting and would match his 'natural gifting' in this area.

As soon as he reached this part of the book he was eager to move on.

However, he decided to continue with the exercises which confirmed and built on his 'Eureka' moment.

This picture triggered Kevin's Eureka moment.

A 'Eureka' moment can come from many places, a photo, a case study etc. It can trigger something which can be a truly wonderful addition to your life.

Watch out for yours!

Recap

In this section we have captured some key career details on your background which might have got you thinking to the point of having your own Eureka moment already.

The next part of our journey helps you to understand why interests are so important.

We meet Oliver and see how they were key for him. It also gives a 'heads up' on how to get the most out of the rest of this book.

Look Forward

WHY ARE WE LOOKING AT YOUR INTERESTS?

In this book we are going to explore your interests, get right inside them if we can, and maybe help you to uncover some more.

Exploring your interests can help you to choose a field of work ...

However, not necessarily the job within the field.

Why are your interests so important?

In terms of your career, interests point you towards the field of work in which you might be happy, for example:

- Finance,
- Medicine,
- Engineering.

Not interested in farming itself, but possibly interested in seeds?

However, you might not necessarily get a job directly within the field in which you are interested. Exploring your interests can help you to choose a field of work, however not necessarily the job within the field.

In other words, you may be interested in farming and though you don't want to be a farmer you may enjoy a job *associated* with farming.

For example, you may be involved with the bookkeeping, marketing, or the selling aspects of running a farm.

... or maybe farm bookkeeping?

Or, researching areas associated within farming from: chemical soil analysis, crop rotation, to analysing the effects of climate change on farming in general.

The key point is that farming in itself *interests* you and you are happy within it.

... or research?

The exploration of what interests you, or could interest you, is therefore a very useful area to explore on our journey together.

... or selling?

Note that interests can cover skills, values and personality traits as well. For example, you may have a skill in computing and be interested in it. Or, you may have the skill (and be very good at it) and not be interested in it— possibly even dislike using it.

You will gain a lot more useful information if you delve into this further. Appendix two page 177 'What exactly are interests? — What should you be looking out for?' will help you if you want to pause and look at it. This is the information I would usually present in one of my workshops.

Skills, like computing, can be interests in themselves as well.

If you do turn to appendix two, please return here afterwards. I will be waiting for you.

Our next port of call is to meet Oliver whose exploration of his interests became his personal breakthrough.

An Insight

I have worked with many people who are in jobs they hate because they are not interested in them.

Sometimes they stay (even though they hate their job), for the money or for a perceived short term gain.

Unfortunately, that 'short term' can end up being 20 years.

CASE STUDY - MEET OLIVER

Oliver made his career change choice just by looking at his interests.

BACKGROUND

Oliver and I started working together, one to one, when he was feeling unfulfilled in his current job and wanted to re-ignite his passion for work.

Oliver was managing a homeless service for 16-25 year olds, and wanted to change his career path to one which was more satisfying. He felt run-down in his job.

Igniting his passion.

For Oliver, it was about rekindling a passion for life and re-igniting his excitement to go to work each day.

He needed help finding out which avenue he should pursue, and wanted guidance on how to achieve his goals.

ACTIONS

Realising where his interests lay.

After only two sessions exploring his interests, Oliver realised that his dream job was to be a make-up artist for film, television and fashion.

Oliver subsequently undertook personality tests and other easy-to-use tools to help him realise the skills and traits he already had, and what he needed to develop in order to achieve his ambitions.

The work was completed by examining a variety of training approaches to help Oliver move forward.

RESULTS

Oliver has since said, "The future looks really bright".

Following his sessions Oliver moved to London to study make-up at the Ealing Film Studios.

Finding out about the training needed.

And seeing it all come true for him.

The course covered make-up, prosthetics, wig-making and facial hair.

A year after he finished, Oliver was able to find work in film, fashion and TV!

He has never looked back.

HOW TO GET THE MOST OUT OF THE OF THIS BOOK

A positive mind-set will help

There are five useful things to keep in mind when reading the book:

Firstly, adopt a positive mind set and be open to new approaches. Our minds can be programmed. If you say 'I want to get the most out of this exercise' your mind will immediately start to look for ways to make that happen.

Secondly, as you work through the book, ideas may come to you.

These may be career ideas or areas you would like to explore further.

Please make a note of these either in your aha! journal (see page 7), or within the notes area on page 244.

These ideas are precious ... They are a way for your subconscious, and your 'wisdom' to send you a message. Capture them.

Look out for ideas on the way.

Please do make use of the journal or the notes area.

Don't let any of those ideas get away!

Give yourself time to think.

Thirdly, work slowly, give yourself time to think.

We rarely give ourselves enough time to think.

Most people spend more time thinking about their next car, holiday or house than they ever do about their careers.

Fourthly, as with all of these exercises, please do find a quiet place to truly think about each question.

Lastly, consider finding a buddy to work through this book with you.

Such a person can really help motivate you.

Finding a partner to review progress with will really help.

Please refer to appendix one page 171 which goes into more detail on the value of such a partner.

When you are ready, turn the page and let us, after a summary, make a start.

SUMMARY

So far we have:

- Started to explore the jungle.
- Carried out some preliminary exercises.
- Met Oliver in a case study.
- Explored why we are looking at your interests.
- Met 'aha' and 'Eureka' moments looking at the difference
- Considered what to do if you have a Eureka' moment.
- Considered how to get the most out of this book
- Introduced the jungle map
- Been introduced to appendices one and two.
- Completed appendix three exercises one to six.
- Been encouraged to start an aha! journal.

Our next move is to start to explore your interests, building up gradually, through a number of exercises, to get you to understand your current interests and maybe generate some new ones on the way.

YOUR CURRENT POSITION ON THE JUNGLE MAP

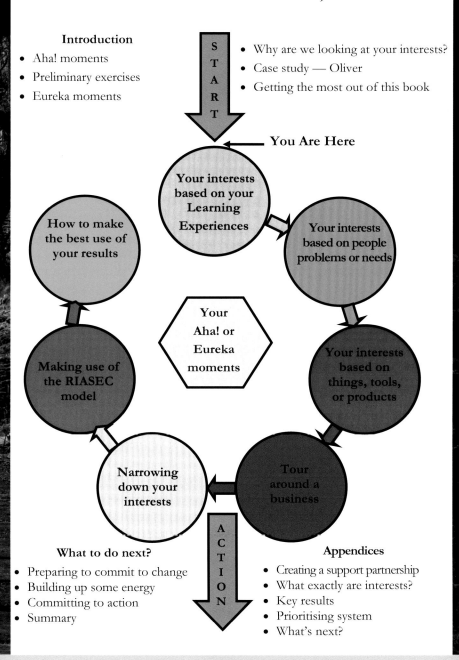

Introduction

- Aha! moments
- Preliminary exercises
- Eureka moments

S T A R T

- Why are we looking at your interests?
- Case study — Oliver
- Getting the most out of this book

You Are Here

Your interests based on your Learning Experiences

How to make the best use of your results

Your interests based on people problems or needs

Your Aha! or Eureka moments

Making use of the RIASEC model

Your interests based on things, tools, or products

Narrowing down your interests

Tour around a business

A C T I O N

What to do next?

- Preparing to commit to change
- Building up some energy
- Committing to action
- Summary

Appendices

- Creating a support partnership
- What exactly are interests?
- Key results
- Prioritising system
- What's next?

Turning theory into reality

Please remember, as with all of these exercises, to find a quiet area and take your time thinking about the questions.

You might find a change of scenery, even just going to a coffee shop, provides a motivating environment which will help you with exercises like this.

Find a quiet, relaxing place to carry out these exercises.

We are initially going to look at four routes into your interests by exploring the following:

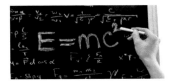

- Interests you have developed from specific learning experiences e.g. school, 'on the Job', Hobbies.

- Interests that involve dealing with people e.g. counseling or consulting.

- Interests that involve things e.g. computers.

- As a complementary approach, the fourth route will ask you to consider the departments in a company within which you might like to work, asking which ones would interest you the most.

Note that the same field of interest may arise from more than one of the areas e.g. Modelling, Building, or Teaching could all lead you to think about Computers or using your hands in some way.

If this happens to you, please enter the interest each time it occurs within the exercise.

The idea here is to create a broad list which we will narrow down later.

We are looking to discover/rediscover some interests and reflect on them.

Having warmed up with the preliminary exercises it is time to move onto the first key exercise.

STEP 1: FINDING INTERESTS FROM LEARNING EXPERIENCES

To start with, complete the tables on the following pages, indicating fields of interest you know something about from the viewpoint of learning experiences.

An example is shown below:

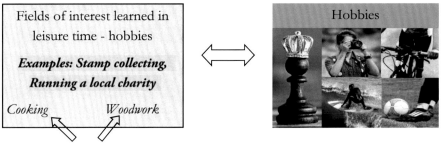

Fields of interest learned in leisure time - hobbies

Examples: Stamp collecting, Running a local charity

Cooking   *Woodwork*

Hobbies

Adding your input where you can - in this example adding 'cooking' and 'woodwork'.

Note, you are not being asked to list everything you have ever studied, we are just after those you have studied and were interested in.

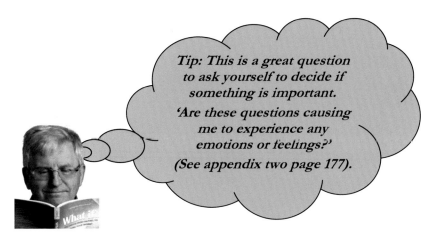

Tip: This is a great question to ask yourself to decide if something is important.

'Are these questions causing me to experience any emotions or feelings?'

(See appendix two page 177).

Fields of interest studied at School, College, University

Examples: *Cooking, French, Computer Science, Physics, Marketing ...*

Your invitation to write something whenever you see the pencil

Fields of interest learned on the job

Examples: *How to operate a milling machine, Lab work, Research ...*

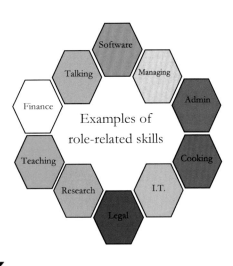

Considering your past.

Fields of interest learned at home - Open University, TV

Examples: Languages, Management ...

Fields of interest learned from training courses, seminars, conferences

Examples: First Aid, Computing Skills ...

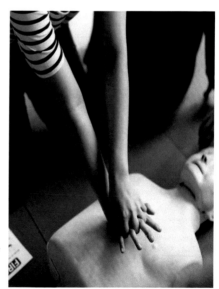

Considering your past.

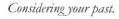

Fields of interest learned
through hobbies

*Examples: Stamp collecting,
Charity work ...*

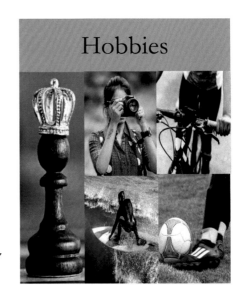

Hobbies

Fields of interest learned from
friends

*Examples: Helping with DIY
projects, working on cars ...*

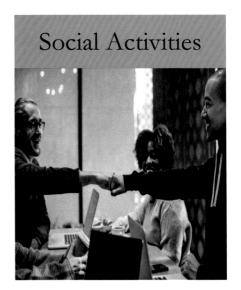

Social Activities

Considering your past.

Now, please pause for a moment.

If you have carried out a few of the other exercises, in say the values or skills books within this series, then you may find that this exercise initially feels quick and easy but please be wary.

It is SO easy to rush through this ... 'At school I was interested in ... say history ... and that's it.'

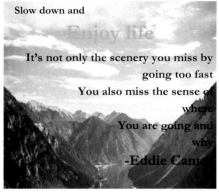

Slow down and

Enjoy life

It's not only the scenery you miss by going too fast
You also miss the sense of where
You are going and why
-Eddie Cant

Thinking about slowing down.

I would, however, encourage you to take your mind back to those days once more ...

Imagine yourself at school, really *remember* what it was like, get inside the emotions and feelings.

Bear in mind that you can take an emotion, think about it and this may lead to a feeling and onto an interest (this is described in more detail in appendix two page 177).

This 'thinking' needs time.

What were you interested in at school?

We don't often consider our past to help our future. Have another look before you move on.

Take time to process it.

Please ensure you have completed Step one (pages 27-31) before moving onto Step two on page 35.

SUMMARY

Let's pause for another summary. In the last section we have:

Explored the things you have learned from a variety of sources.

- School, College, University.
- On the job.
- Learned at home.

The next part of the journey is going to explore your people interests.

YOUR CURRENT POSITION ON THE JUNGLE MAP

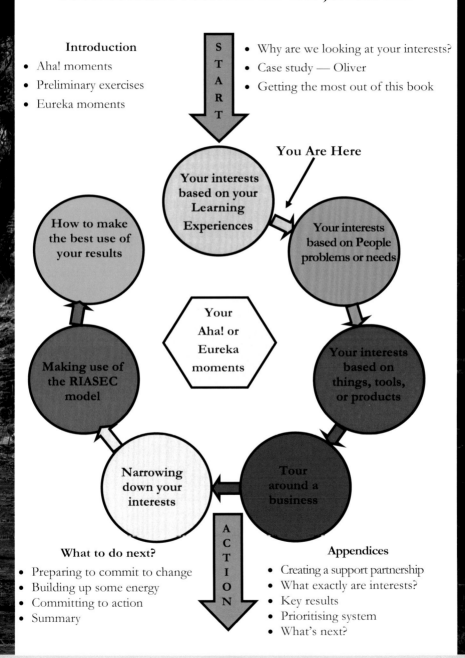

Introduction
- Aha! moments
- Preliminary exercises
- Eureka moments

START

- Why are we looking at your interests?
- Case study — Oliver
- Getting the most out of this book

You Are Here

Your interests based on your Learning Experiences

Your interests based on People problems or needs

How to make the best use of your results

Your Aha! or Eureka moments

Making use of the RIASEC model

Your interests based on things, tools, or products

Narrowing down your interests

Tour around a business

ACTION

What to do next?
- Preparing to commit to change
- Building up some energy
- Committing to action
- Summary

Appendices
- Creating a support partnership
- What exactly are interests?
- Key results
- Prioritising system
- What's next?

Taking the next step on our journey.

STEP 2: FINDING INTERESTS DEALING WITH PEOPLE, PROBLEMS OR NEEDS

Step one looked at your interests from the point of view of things you have studied/learned.

Step two, moves on to look specifically at fields of interests connected with people and their needs. You may have already covered some of these within the first part, however, by looking at your interests from a variety of angles we ensure, as far as possible, we do not miss anything.

We will be looking at people ....

Over the next few pages are photos and titles of careers involving working directly with people in some way.

Please ⃝circle any which you find are of interest to you - NOTE please ignore the fact that you may not have any experience, or training, within the areas. It is your interests alone that we are looking at here

Which areas concerned with people problems or needs interest you?

Please let your eyes rest on each of them and imagine being there.

Space has been left for you to capture any other interests which occur to you at the end of the exercise on page 55.

Just before you start, it is really important to reinforce an earlier message.

Hundreds of people have completed this exercise (or one very much like it) and there is something *which nearly always happens*.

Far too often people rush it. They glance at the areas and rush on. Maybe it is something to do with human nature, we miss so much in life by rushing.

I wish we were in a 1:1 session right now to encourage you to slow down and let

In my experience, every time you manage to slow down, something magical happens leading to new discoveries. Give yourself time to think.

Remember that you are not being asked if you have any skills, qualifications or experience in these particular areas.

Please look at each area and ask:

- Am I drawn to this area at all?
- Would I be interested to work in an area where this is happening? Ok, I may not actually be doing what is shown in the picture e.g. Selling clothing however, I may be working in some support capacity (e.g. Buying). If so circle it.

Additionally, make notes of any thoughts which occur to you in the spaces provided.

This can really pay dividends.

See examples here.

Some examples of completing the tables in the exercise..

Clothing	Not selling or making Clothing, perhaps as a buyer?
Family/Consumer Economics	Possibly counselling?
Info. Technology	Maybe writing about it.

PLEASE CIRCLE THOSE WHICH INTEREST YOU.

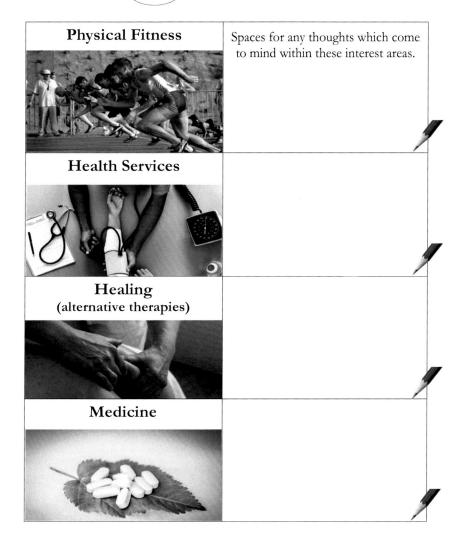

Physical Fitness	Spaces for any thoughts which come to mind within these interest areas.
Health Services	
Healing (alternative therapies)	
Medicine	

Do people related interests figure within your career?

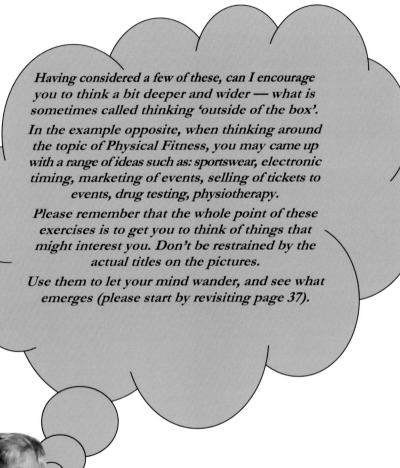

Having considered a few of these, can I encourage you to think a bit deeper and wider — what is sometimes called thinking 'outside of the box'.

In the example opposite, when thinking around the topic of Physical Fitness, you may came up with a range of ideas such as: sportswear, electronic timing, marketing of events, selling of tickets to events, drug testing, physiotherapy.

Please remember that the whole point of these exercises is to get you to think of things that might interest you. Don't be restrained by the actual titles on the pictures.

Use them to let your mind wander, and see what emerges (please start by revisiting page 37).

PLEASE(CIRCLE)THOSE WHICH INTEREST YOU.

Physical fitness 	Spaces for any thoughts which come to mind within these interest areas. • *Maybe selling sportswear,* • *Involved in the organisation,* • *making the electronic measurement equipment,* • *Physiotherapy*
Clothing 	
Food 	
Housing 	

PLEASE CIRCLE THOSE WHICH INTEREST YOU.

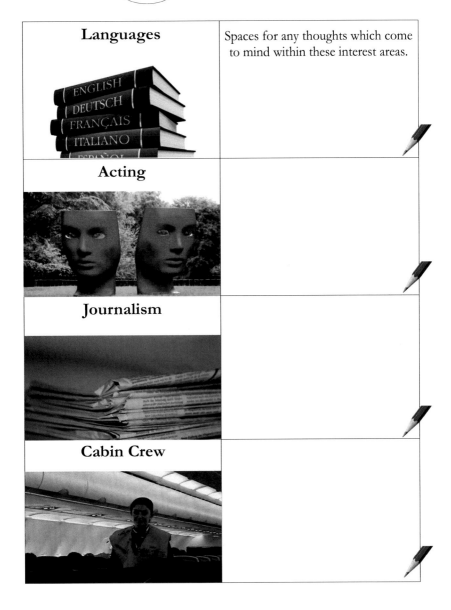

Languages	Spaces for any thoughts which come to mind within these interest areas.
Acting	
Journalism	
Cabin Crew	

PLEASE (CIRCLE) THOSE WHICH INTEREST YOU.

Personal Services	Spaces for any thoughts which come to mind within these interest areas.
Family/Consumer Economics	
Retail Sales	
Car Sales	

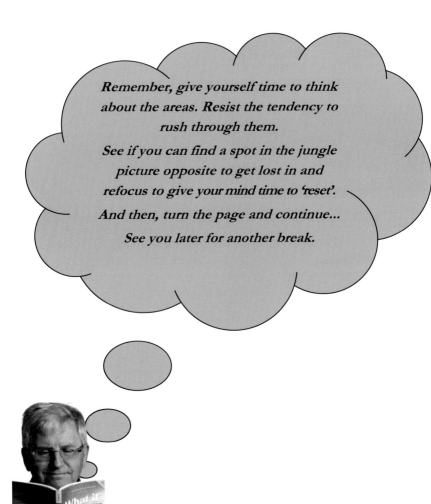

Remember, give yourself time to think about the areas. Resist the tendency to rush through them.

See if you can find a spot in the jungle picture opposite to get lost in and refocus to give your mind time to 'reset'.

And then, turn the page and continue...

See you later for another break.

Find a place to recharge.

PLEASE CIRCLE THOSE WHICH INTEREST YOU.

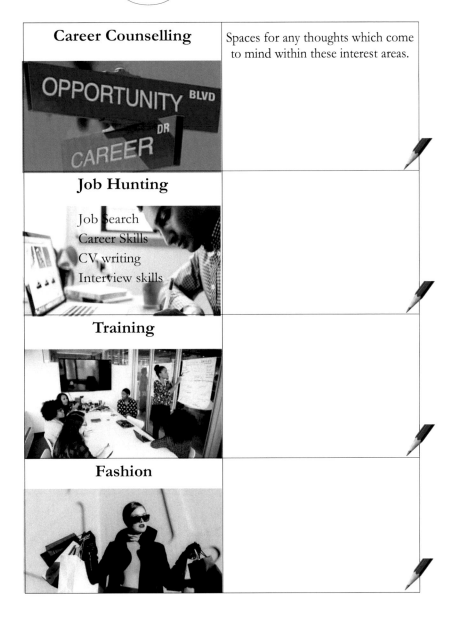

Career Counselling	Spaces for any thoughts which come to mind within these interest areas.
Job Hunting Job Search Career Skills CV writing Interview skills	
Training	
Fashion	

PLEASE CIRCLE THOSE WHICH INTEREST YOU.

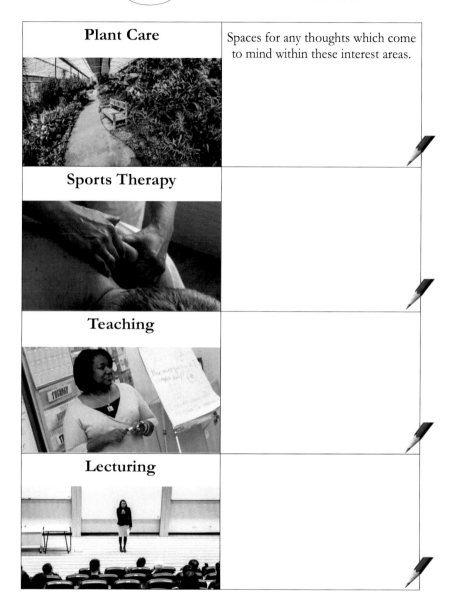

Plant Care	Spaces for any thoughts which come to mind within these interest areas.
Sports Therapy	
Teaching	
Lecturing	

PLEASE CIRCLE THOSE WHICH INTEREST YOU.

Legal Services

Child Development

Entertainment

Religion

Please (CIRCLE) THOSE WHICH INTEREST YOU.

Animal Care 	Spaces for any thoughts which come to mind within these interest areas.
Mental Health 	
Psychology 	
Personal Counselling	

I wonder where you will pause this time?

PLEASE CIRCLE THOSE WHICH INTEREST YOU.

Emergency Services 	Spaces for any thoughts which come to mind within these interest areas.
Social Work 	
Public Services 	
Charity Careers 	

PLEASE CIRCLE THOSE WHICH INTEREST YOU.

Financial Services 	Spaces for any thoughts which come to mind within these interest areas.
Info. Technology 	
The Armed Forces 	
Dietician 	

PLEASE CIRCLE THOSE WHICH INTEREST YOU.

Beautician 	Spaces for any thoughts which come to mind within these interest areas.
Police Officer 	
Politician 	
Dentist 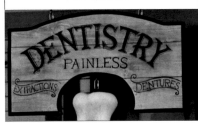	

PLEASE CIRCLE THOSE WHICH INTEREST YOU.

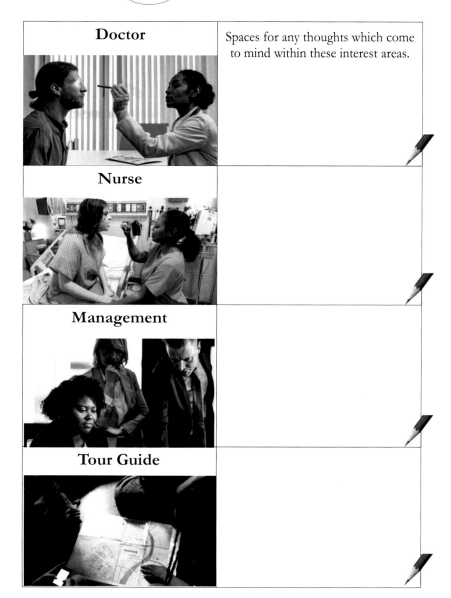

Doctor	Spaces for any thoughts which come to mind within these interest areas.
Nurse	
Management	
Tour Guide	

PLEASE CIRCLE THOSE WHICH INTEREST YOU.

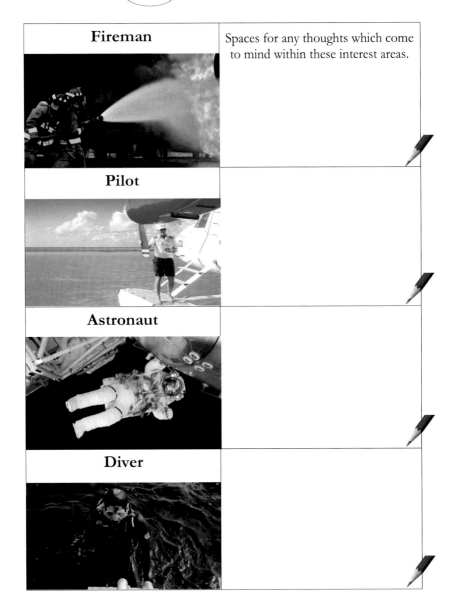

Fireman

Spaces for any thoughts which come to mind within these interest areas.

Pilot

Astronaut

Diver

PLEASE CIRCLE THOSE WHICH INTEREST YOU.

What are your other People related interests?	Spaces for any thoughts which come to mind within these interest areas.
Any more?	
Any more?	
Any more?	

Time for another break in the jungle?

Shortly, we will be moving onto another exercise to explore another angle.

Before we do, please now go back to the previous exercise (starting on page 37) and star (*) the three you are most interested in before we move on. This will help you with prioritising your interests later

Please ensure you have completed Step 2 before moving onto Step 3.

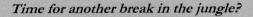

Time to recharge again.

SUMMARY

Let's pause for another summary. In the last section we have:

- Looked at your people related interests.

> *The next part of our journey is to explore areas of interest associated with 'Things, Tools or Products'.*

YOUR CURRENT POSITION ON THE JUNGLE MAP

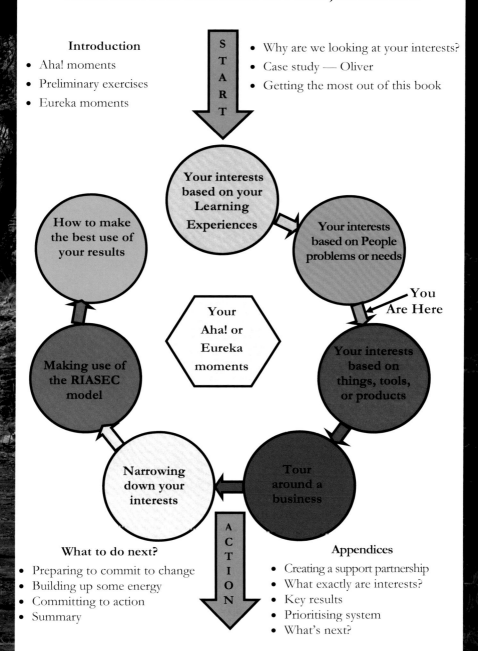

Introduction
- Aha! moments
- Preliminary exercises
- Eureka moments

START

- Why are we looking at your interests?
- Case study — Oliver
- Getting the most out of this book

Your interests based on your Learning Experiences

How to make the best use of your results

Your interests based on People problems or needs

Your Aha! or Eureka moments

You Are Here

Making use of the RIASEC model

Your interests based on things, tools, or products

Narrowing down your interests

Tour around a business

ACTION

What to do next?
- Preparing to commit to change
- Building up some energy
- Committing to action
- Summary

Appendices
- Creating a support partnership
- What exactly are interests?
- Key results
- Prioritising system
- What's next?

Making progress - onto the Next Step - Things, Tools or Products.

STEP 3: FINDING INTERESTS DEALING WITH THINGS, TOOLS OR PRODUCTS

Having looked at your people based interests we are now moving onto looking at material things.

Keep
going,
You are
getting
there.

As with the last exercise, there now follows a selection of titles and photos to help you consider those which you are drawn to.

As an example, which areas associated with space travel interest you?

Please remember, it is not to do with whether you have the skills or experience to carry these out - we are just looking for the ones you are interested in.

A reminder, and a little more explanation on this.

The importance of identifying your interests (even if you could never consider a job directly within those interest areas) is that:

- You may get a job associated with it for example for space travel, you might work within a support area, for instance: security or hospitality.

- Identifying areas in which you are interested in may trigger other areas as well.

Circle all you are interested in. Please ignore how impossible they may seem.

Your Ideas

Space has been left for the inclusion of any other interests which occur to you at the end of the exercise on page 83.

PLEASE CIRCLE THOSE WHICH INTEREST YOU.

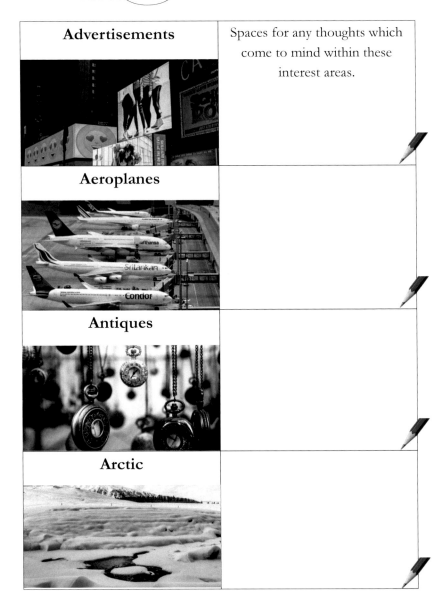

Advertisements	Spaces for any thoughts which come to mind within these interest areas.
Aeroplanes	
Antiques	
Arctic	

Please remember to continue to think outside of the box.

Don't let the actual picture or the title define your thinking.

See what ideas the pictures and/or titles can generate, all ideas are helpful if they interest you. Any of them might lead to a career.

Please see the example opposite.

It is amazing how ideas emerge if you let them. See the ideas that came to me after simply looking at the picture on the next page.

PLEASE CIRCLE THOSE WHICH INTEREST YOU.

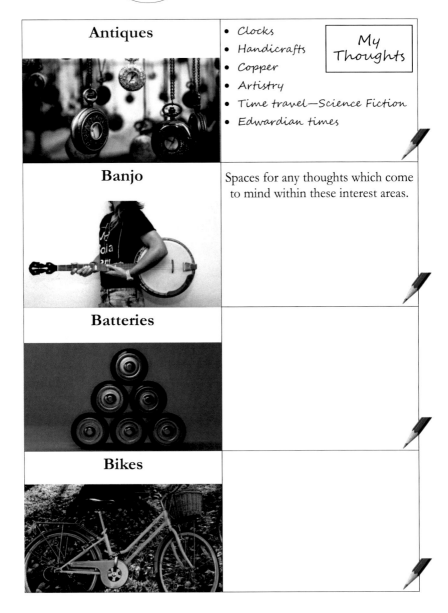

Antiques

- Clocks
- Handicrafts
- Copper
- Artistry
- Time travel—Science Fiction
- Edwardian times

My Thoughts

Banjo

Spaces for any thoughts which come to mind within these interest areas.

Batteries

Bikes

Please (CIRCLE) THOSE WHICH INTEREST YOU.

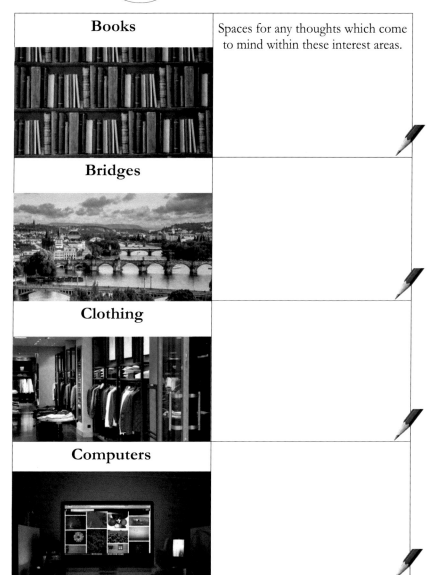

Books	Spaces for any thoughts which come to mind within these interest areas.
Bridges	
Clothing	
Computers	

PLEASE CIRCLE THOSE WHICH INTEREST YOU.

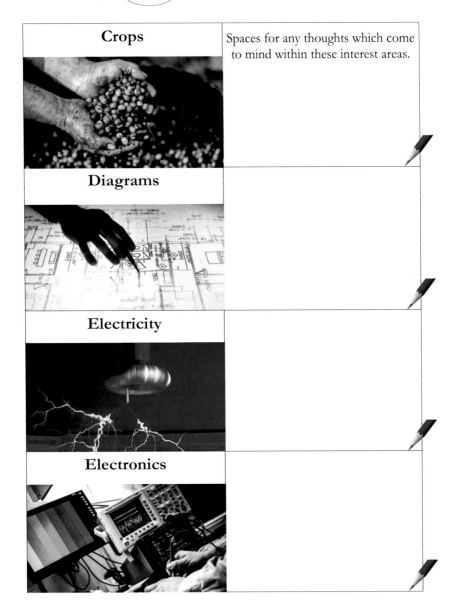

Crops	Spaces for any thoughts which come to mind within these interest areas.
Diagrams	
Electricity	
Electronics	

PLEASE CIRCLE THOSE WHICH INTEREST YOU.

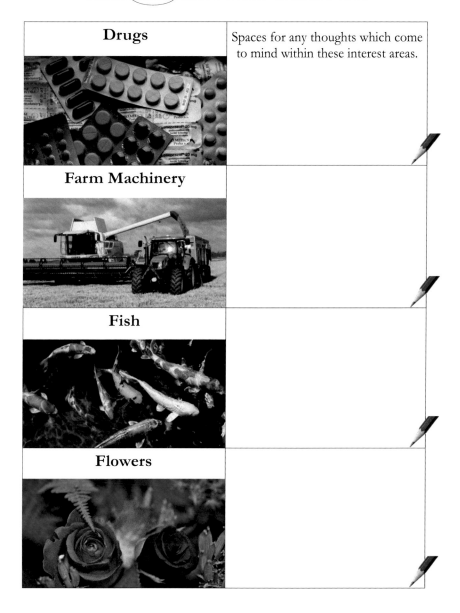

Drugs	Spaces for any thoughts which come to mind within these interest areas.
Farm Machinery	
Fish	
Flowers	

Time to recharge again.

PLEASE CIRCLE THOSE WHICH INTEREST YOU.

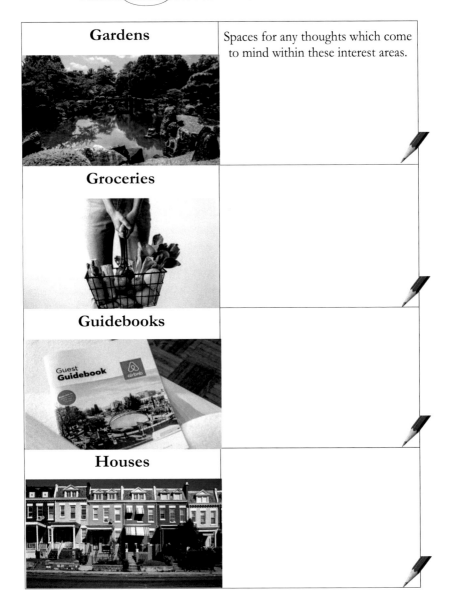

| **Gardens** | Spaces for any thoughts which come to mind within these interest areas. |

Groceries

Guidebooks

Houses

PLEASE CIRCLE THOSE WHICH INTEREST YOU.

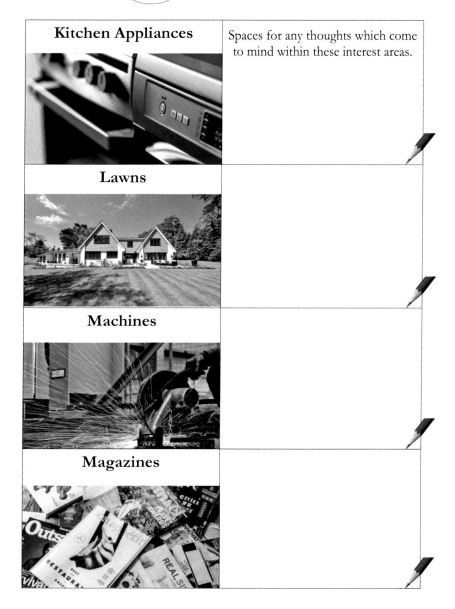

Kitchen Appliances

Spaces for any thoughts which come to mind within these interest areas.

Lawns

Machines

Magazines

PLEASE CIRCLE THOSE WHICH INTEREST YOU.

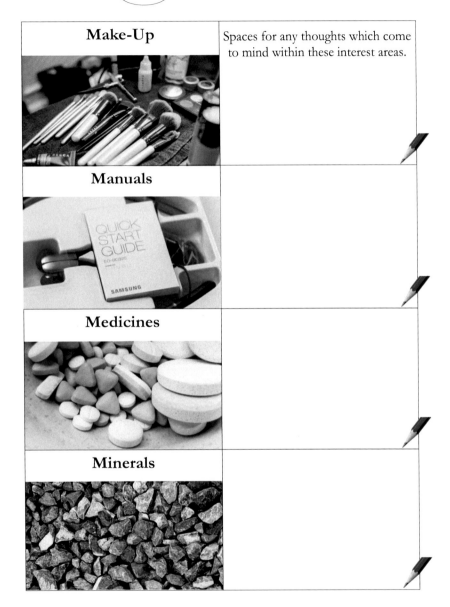

Make-Up	Spaces for any thoughts which come to mind within these interest areas.
Manuals	
Medicines	
Minerals	

PLEASE (CIRCLE) THOSE WHICH INTEREST YOU.

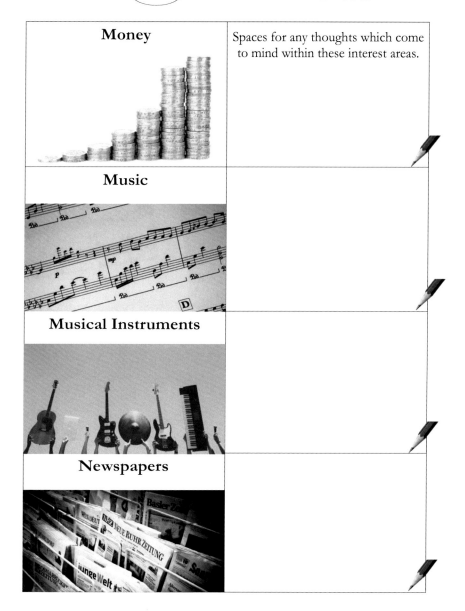

Money	Spaces for any thoughts which come to mind within these interest areas.
Music	
Musical Instruments	
Newspapers	

Rest by the waterfall for a while.

I have actually been here, by the way, and stood on the viewing platform in the middle — Why don't you join me there?

It's a beautiful place to recharge and think about what could be.

When you are ready, turn the page and continue.

See you later for another break.

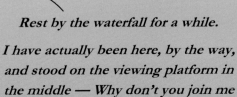

Iguazu Falls - Brazil

Time to recharge again.

PLEASE (CIRCLE) THOSE WHICH INTEREST YOU.

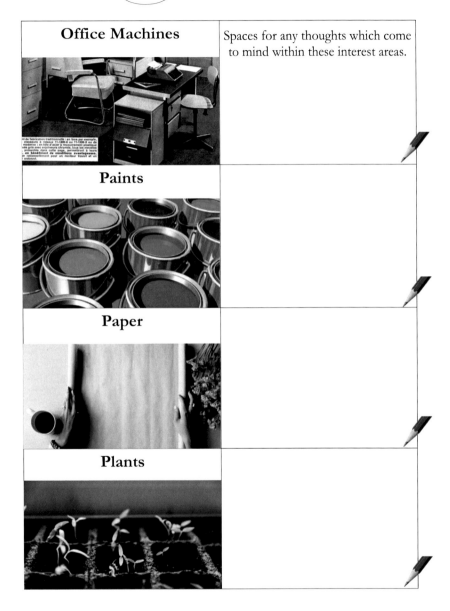

Office Machines	Spaces for any thoughts which come to mind within these interest areas.
Paints	
Paper	
Plants	

PLEASE CIRCLE THOSE WHICH INTEREST YOU.

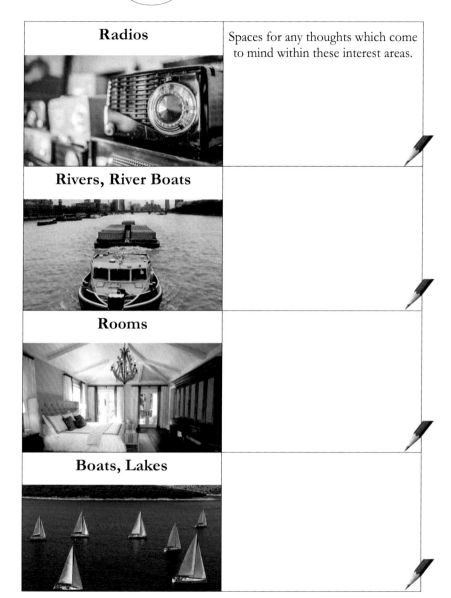

Radios

Spaces for any thoughts which come to mind within these interest areas.

Rivers, River Boats

Rooms

Boats, Lakes

PLEASE (CIRCLE) THOSE WHICH INTEREST YOU.

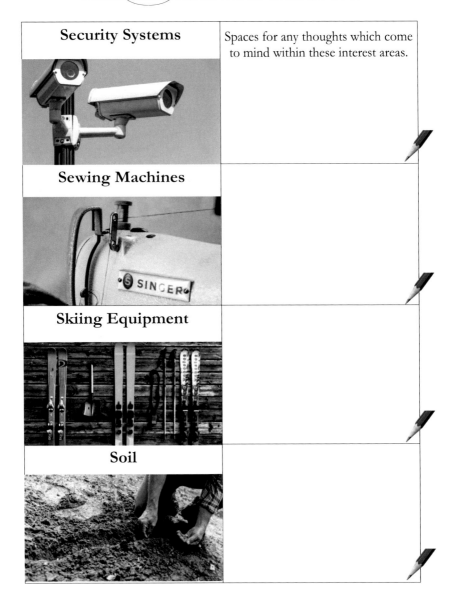

Security Systems	Spaces for any thoughts which come to mind within these interest areas.
Sewing Machines	
Skiing Equipment	
Soil	

PLEASE (CIRCLE) THOSE WHICH INTEREST YOU.

Telephones	Spaces for any thoughts which come to mind within these interest areas.
Toiletries	
Tools	
Toys	

PLEASE CIRCLE THOSE WHICH INTEREST YOU.

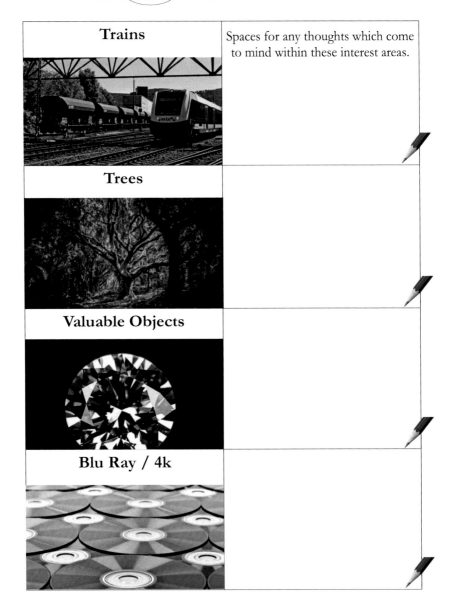

Trains	Spaces for any thoughts which come to mind within these interest areas.
Trees	
Valuable Objects	
Blu Ray / 4k	

PLEASE CIRCLE THOSE WHICH INTEREST YOU.

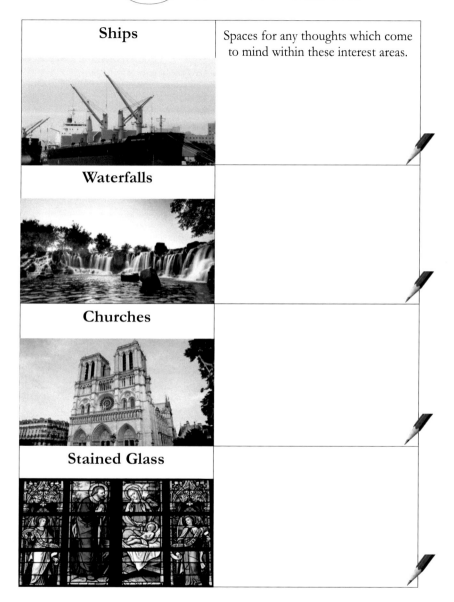

Ships	Spaces for any thoughts which come to mind within these interest areas.
Waterfalls	
Churches	
Stained Glass	

PLEASE CIRCLE THOSE WHICH INTEREST YOU.

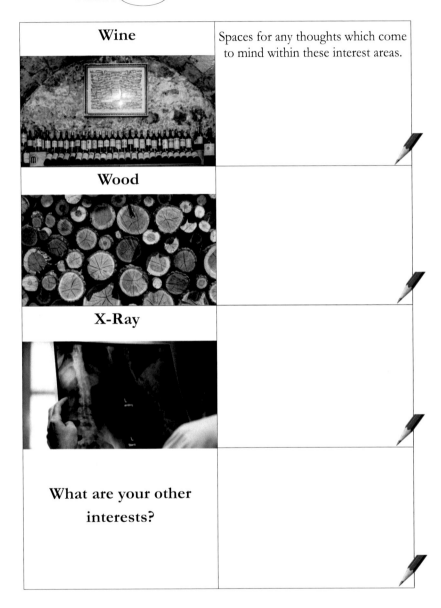

Wine	Spaces for any thoughts which come to mind within these interest areas.
Wood	
X-Ray	
What are your other interests?	

PLEASE (CIRCLE) THOSE WHICH INTEREST YOU.

Any others?	Spaces for any thoughts which come to mind within these interest areas.
Any others?	
Any others?	

Now, return to the start on page 62 and mark with an asterix *
the three in which you are most interested.

(Again this will help when you prioritise your interests later).

Have a break if you need it.

SUMMARY

Let's pause for another summary. In the last section we have:

- Explored your interests associated with 'Things, Tools or Products'.

> *The next part of our journey is to take a 'flight of fancy' by looking inside a fictitious company and seeing which departments you are drawn to.*

YOUR CURRENT POSITION ON THE JUNGLE MAP

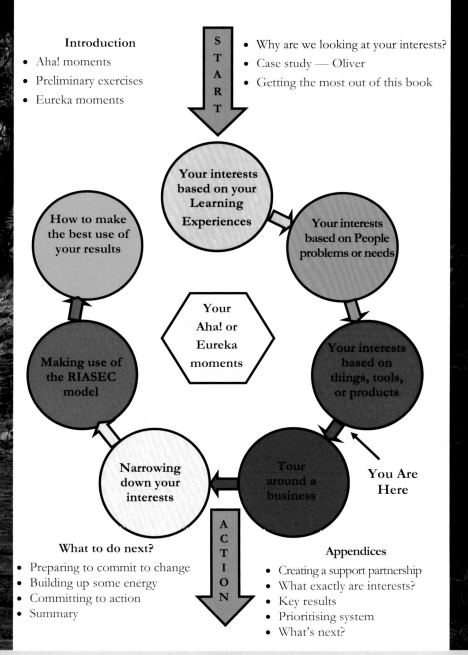

Introduction
- Aha! moments
- Preliminary exercises
- Eureka moments

START

- Why are we looking at your interests?
- Case study — Oliver
- Getting the most out of this book

Your interests based on your Learning Experiences

How to make the best use of your results

Your interests based on People problems or needs

Your Aha! or Eureka moments

Making use of the RIASEC model

Your interests based on things, tools, or products

Narrowing down your interests

Tour around a business

You Are Here

ACTION

What to do next?
- Preparing to commit to change
- Building up some energy
- Committing to action
- Summary

Appendices
- Creating a support partnership
- What exactly are interests?
- Key results
- Prioritising system
- What's next?

Another chance to escape the jungle for a while.

STEP 4:   A DAY OUT—TAKING A TOUR AROUND AN EXCITING BUSINESS

Gaining ideas from a typical business.

On pages 90 to 95 are a number of 'floor plans' representing component parts of a typical business.

This exercise is to imagine you are spending a day touring the business getting to know how it works and meeting the people.

As you look at the floor plans *see if you can slow right down* and imagine you are walking around talking to the people.

Try and visualise touring the business ... and as you do, ask yourself:

- Which areas am I drawn to?
- What types of work can I see myself doing within the company?
- Are you working inside the business or outside in some capacity?

Being greeted to look around.

Ring the areas which interest you and add any notes.

The objective is to ring the areas which interest you and maybe capture some notes on the diagrams.

Remember, those which give rise to an emotion or feeling will give you a clue (see appendix two on page 177).

Enjoy your stay!

Just a thought ... If it were your company, which roles would you like to do yourself and which would you employ others to do?

Arriving for the tour.

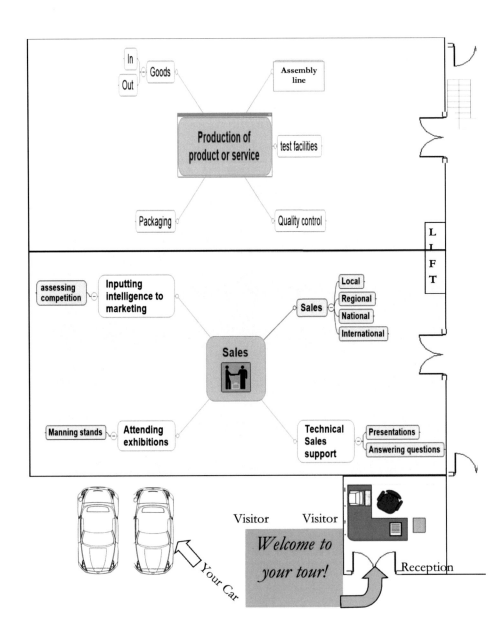

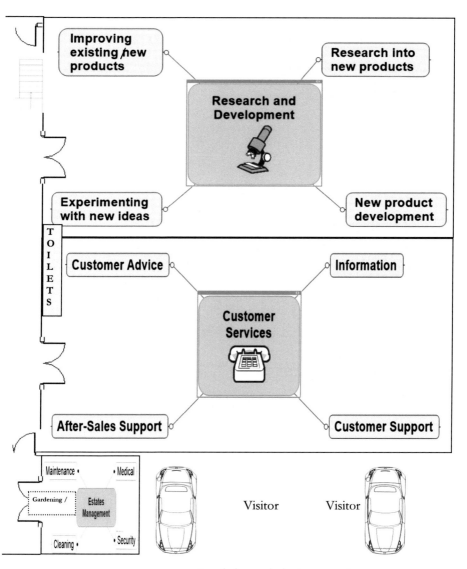

Improving existing /new products

Research into new products

Research and Development

Experimenting with new ideas

New product development

TOILETS

Customer Advice

Information

Customer Services

After-Sales Support

Customer Support

Maintenance •   • Medical

Gardening /   Estates Management

Cleaning •   • Security

Visitor   Visitor

As we look around what interests you?

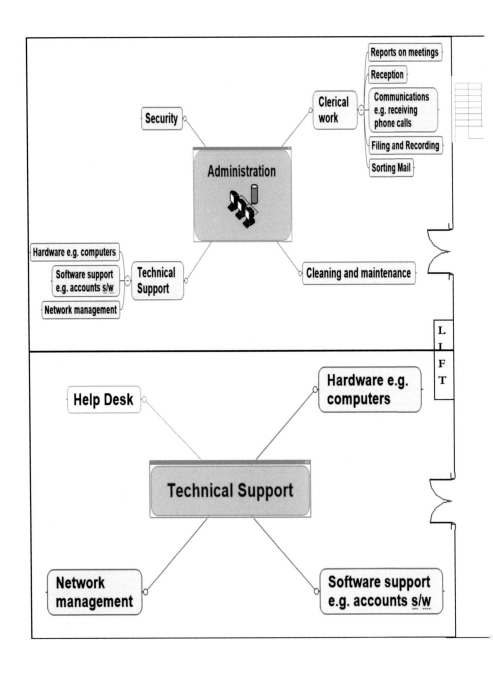

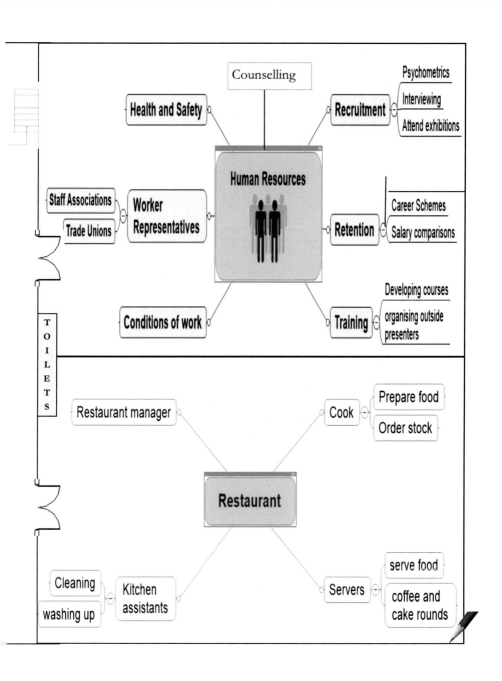

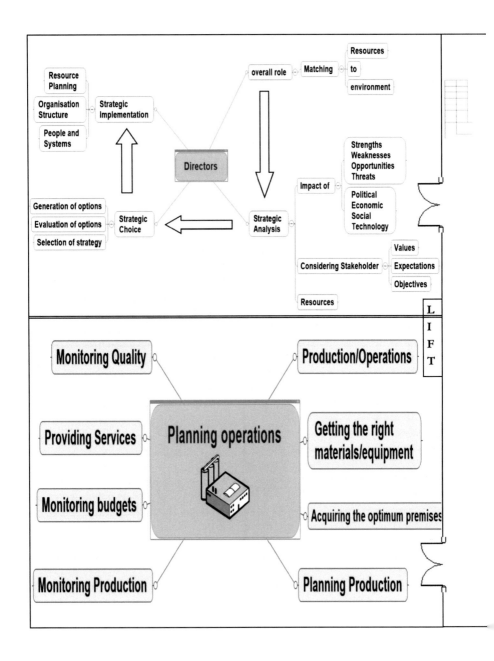

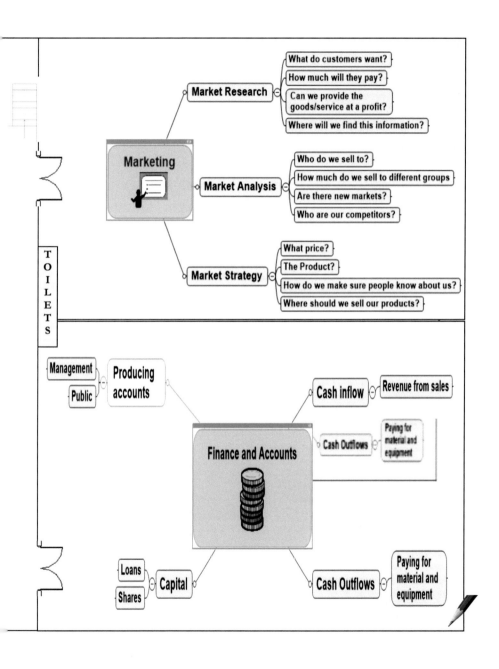

SUMMARY

Let's pause for another summary. In this section we have:

- Been invited into a fictitious company to explore which departments, if any, you might be interested in working for.

> The next part of our journey is to review interests from all of the four approaches, together with the preliminary exercises, and to decide which attract you the most.

YOUR CURRENT POSITION ON THE JUNGLE MAP

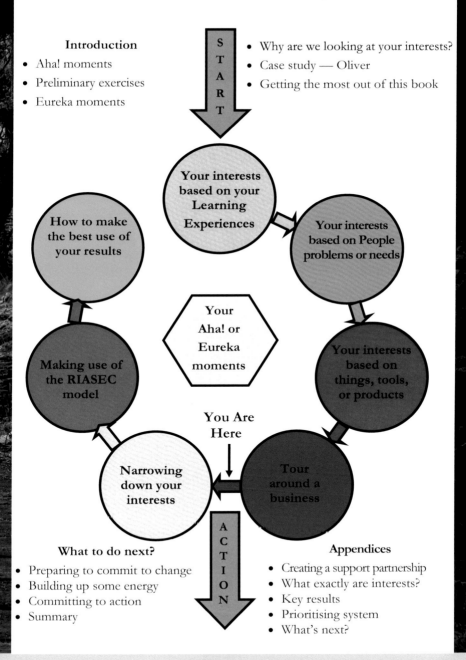

Introduction
- Aha! moments
- Preliminary exercises
- Eureka moments

START

- Why are we looking at your interests?
- Case study — Oliver
- Getting the most out of this book

Your interests based on your **Learning Experiences**

How to make the best use of your results

Your interests based on People problems or needs

Your **Aha!** or **Eureka** moments

Making use of the RIASEC model

Your interests based on things, tools, or products

You Are Here

Narrowing down your interests

Tour around a business

ACTION

What to do next?
- Preparing to commit to change
- Building up some energy
- Committing to action
- Summary

Appendices
- Creating a support partnership
- What exactly are interests?
- Key results
- Prioritising system
- What's next?

Pausing to collect your thoughts.

STEP 5: NARROWING DOWN YOUR INTERESTS

Having now looked at your interests from four different points of view, our next step is to decide which ones you find the most interesting.

To do this, please can you make a few photocopies of page 104 and cut into cards, or get a stack of post-its and on each one write the heading of one of the interests you have found from the exercises (example opposite).

We have now looked at your interests from four different points of view.

Please don't forget to include any career ideas generated from preliminary exercises one to six (pages 188 to 205).

If any other interests come to mind as you complete this, please add them.

Please then select the top 25 from your selection and prioritise from most interesting to least.

Electronics	Counselling
Teaching	Sailing
Business	Researching

Example of what we are looking for.

If you are struggling to prioritise, there are two tools which might help you which my 1:1 clients find particularly useful.

A simple tool which is presented on the next two pages and a more difficult one which is in appendix four page 219. I encourage you to use the one in appendix four, however, it will take you longer. If you don't need help turn to page 102.

PRIORITISING TOOL

This tool works by picking up each card, (or post-it) one at a time, and deciding its priority against one of a set of categories ranging from 'relatively most important' to 'relatively least important'. Whilst you can carry out this exercise quite quickly, it can be thought-provoking and I really suggest you set aside about 30 minutes with a large cup of coffee. Detailed instructions follow:

Step one: If you haven't already done so, you will need a number of cards or post-it notes. Put one interest on each card, or post-it note and place them in a pile.

Step two: Produce five more cards, or post-its, labeled as shown below (relatively most important to relatively least important, graduated 5 to 1).

Step three: Arrange your cards against the five headings (you may possibly have many more than I am showing here).

At this stage do not spend too long thinking about it, just place them fairly quickly.

Step four: Move the cards around until you have roughly the same amount of post-its in each column.

As you do this, other interests may come to mind. If they do simply add them in the appropriate category.

Step five: Select the top 25 cards, and lay them out in front of you.

Step six: Leave them for a while and then return and consider if they are in the right order, and if not reorder until you are satisfied.

Taking your top 25, lay them out on the table in front of you from left to right. Arrange them by priority, moving them around until you are happy with their relative positions (if you have used the priortising tool on page 100 this will have been done for you).

If you didn't use the tool on page 100 and you find that prioritising the 25 is too large a number to work with, please return to page 100, for help.

Having decided the priority of your top 25 please enter them onto the table on page 103.

Interest Area (up to 25)	Priority Review date			
	Initial date	1	2	3
(columns "Review 1-3" have been included to allow you to re-prioritise at a later date if you want to)	10 aug 18	12 jan 2021	24 feb 2022	12 sept 2023
Electronics	1	1	2	1
Psychology	2	4	1	2
Counselling	3	2	4	3
Cooking	4	3	3	4

You can see an example here where my own first four interests were electronics, psychology, counselling, and cooking which got priorities 1,2,3 and 4. I wonder what yours will work out to be?

Note the presence of the other columns. These allow you to re-prioritise at another date if you want to later in your career.

Interest Area (up to 25)	Priority			
(1 = most interesting, 25 = least interesting)	Initial Date	Review 1	Review 2	Review 3
(columns 'Review 1-3' have been included to allow you to re-prioritise at a later date if you want to)				
	1			
	2			
	3			
	4			
	5			
	6			
	7			
	8			
	9			
	10			
	11			
	12			
	13			
	14			
	15			
	16			
	17			
	18			
	19			
	20			
	21			
	22			
	23			
	24			
	25			

Sorted your cards? Let's move on.

MILESTONE

We have reached a milestone on our journey together! Our next step is to use another effective, however different, approach and then later bring the two approaches together.

SUMMARY

Let's pause for another summary. In the last section we have:

- Condensed your interests down to a selection of 25.

The next part of our journey is to look at a specific approach which is used world wide.

YOUR CURRENT POSITION ON THE JUNGLE MAP

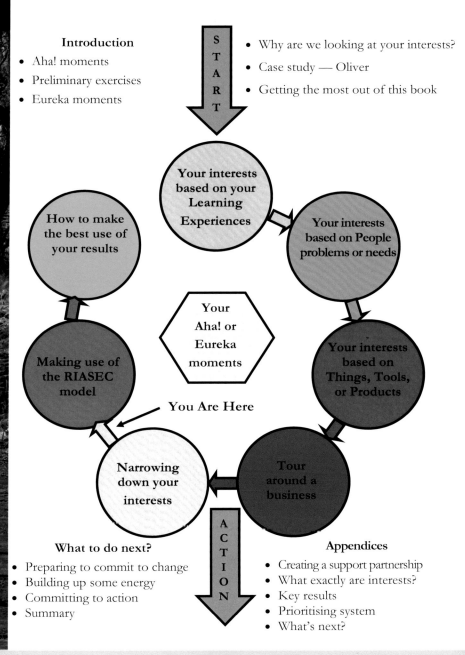

Introduction
- Aha! moments
- Preliminary exercises
- Eureka moments

START

- Why are we looking at your interests?
- Case study — Oliver
- Getting the most out of this book

Your interests based on your **Learning Experiences**

How to make the best use of your results

Your interests based on People problems or needs

Your Aha! or Eureka moments

Making use of the RIASEC model

Your interests based on Things, Tools, or Products

You Are Here

Narrowing down your interests

Tour around a business

ACTION

What to do next?
- Preparing to commit to change
- Building up some energy
- Committing to action
- Summary

Appendices
- Creating a support partnership
- What exactly are interests?
- Key results
- Prioritising system
- What's next?

Meeting with John Holland in Step 6 to delve deeper into six specific interest areas.

Step 6: Applying John Holland's RIASEC model to your situation

The next part of our journey is to meet John Holland who produced a very effective model known as his RIASEC career model. Together with associated career tools, these have been very popular over the last few decades, producing a number of resources directly matching people to careers which might suit them. His model is based on the view that our interests fall into a mixture of the following six categories:

Area	Examples
1 **Realistic (R)** (e.g. building)	
2 **Investigative (I)** (e.g. police investigator)	
3 **Artistic (A)** (e.g. sculpture work)	
4 **Social (S)** (e.g. interviewer)	
5 **Entrepreneurial (E)** (e.g. speculator)	
6 **Conventional (C)** (e.g. accountancy)	

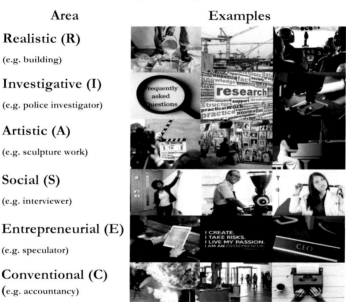

Holland's six different interest areas.

The model works by identifying your top one, two or three interest areas to produce your RIASEC code, for example R (on its own), EC, or SIA, and from these identify a number of careers.

There are many places you can get a RIASEC or, sometimes called, HOLLAND assessment if you wish to pursue this further, either via a career consultant or online. I regularly use them with my clients. To get you started however, two approaches have been included here to allow you to get an idea of what your code might be and to use it within this book. Turn the page for an example of the first approach then it is your go.

In this exercise please read the cells adjacent to the areas below, (circle) those you relate to, and using the last cell, rate yourself against the area. Having completed them decide which are your top three and copy them into the three boxes to the right at the top of the next page (please note that only four of the six RIASEC areas are shown due to the space on the page, the full six are in the exercise when you turn over).

You can see in the example below, I started by circling areas which resonated with me.

Area	I have preferences for careers Involving...	My Values (there is a separate book in the series to explore these further if you are interested)	I see myself in the following way...
Realistic (R)	• Machines • Tools • 'Hands on' • Strength	• Reward for the work done	• Practical • Mechanical skills
Investigative (I)	• Understanding things • Exploring • Researching	• Gaining knowledge for its own sake	• Analytical
Artistic (A)	• Music • Art • Poetry	• Creating things	• Innovative • Creative
Social (S)	• Care giving • Teaching • Explaining	• Helping others	• Patient

Having done this, I considered them against each other to arrive at the Xs on the lines in the last column. It was then simply a case of transferring the appropriate letters to the boxes in the right-hand corner in my case: S, A, I. (to be clear it is the rating in the last column that leads to the actual code as you can see by the dashed arrows).

My RIASEC code is ⟶

1st	2nd	3rd
S	A	I

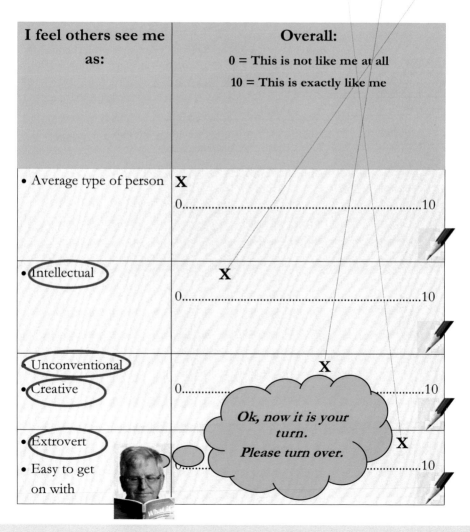

I feel others see me as:	Overall: 0 = This is not like me at all 10 = This is exactly like me
• Average type of person	X 0..10
• Intellectual	X 0..10
Unconventional • Creative	X 0..10
• Extrovert • Easy to get on with	X 0..10

Ok, now it is your turn.
Please turn over.

In this exercise please read the cells adjacent to the six areas below, (circle) those you relate to, and using the last cell, rate yourself against the area. Having completed all six decide which are your top three and copy them into the three boxes to the right.

Area	I have preferences for careers Involving...	My Values (there is a separate book in the series to explore these further if you are interested)	I see myself in the following way...
Realistic (R)	• Machines • Tools • 'Hands on' • Strength	• Reward for the work done	• Practical • Mechanical skills
Investigative (I)	• Understanding things • Exploring • Researching	• Gaining knowledge for its own sake	• Analytical • Independent
Artistic (A)	• Music • Art • Poetry	• Creating things	• Innovative • Creative
Social (S)	• Care giving • Teaching • Explaining	• Helping others	• Patient • Good Listener
Entrepreneurial(E)	• Influencing • Controlling • Leading	• Achieving things • Social status	• Persuasive • Motivating
Conventional(C)	• Routine • Standards	• Order in things	• Organised • Methodical

My RIASEC code is ———→

1st	2nd	3rd

I feel others see me as:	Overall: 0 = This is not like me at all 10 = This is exactly like me
• Average type of person • "Hands on" • Enjoys using tools/machinery	0..10
• Intellectual • A "Thinker" • Curious	0..10
• Unconventional • Creative • Innovative	0..10
• Extrovert • Easy to get on with • A Natural helper	0..10
• Energetic • Risk Taker • A Leader	0..10
• Careful • Detailed • A "Finisher"	0..10

Armed with the knowledge of your RIASEC code, there are a number of resources which you can use to look up the careers suited to your code.

The Dictionary of Holland Occupational Codes is such a resource and a selection for the SAE and SER codes is shown on the next page.

Using the six areas to research further.

Please note that if you can't quite decide between two codes, say ISA and ISR (another pair of code examples), then it is a good idea to look up both of the codes.

The RIASEC code has been used for years to help match people against careers: putting the right people in the right places.

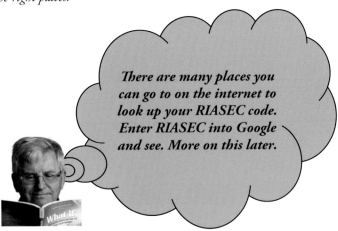

There are many places you can go to on the internet to look up your RIASEC code. Enter RIASEC into Google and see. More on this later.

From Holland codes to the directory of occupational titles occupations

The RIASEC code is often abbreviated HOC (Holland Occupational Code)

HOC	Title
SAE	Musical therapist
SAE	Graduate assistant (education)
SAE	Councillor (professional)
SAE	Councillor, marriage and family
SAE	Art therapist
SAE	Director, instructional material
SAE	Food and drug inspector
SAE	Teacher Elementary School
SAE	Teacher secondary school
SAE	Teacher preschool
SAE	Nursery school attendant
SER	Director educational community health
SER	Director, institution (any industry)
SER	Administrator, Healthcare facility
SER	Director, agricultural services
SER	Director, consumer affairs
SER	Director, licensing and registration
SER	Asst Branch manager financial institution
SER	Commissioner, public works

REFINING YOUR RIASEC CODE

The key to our RIASEC journey together is to see how accurately we can identify your code. Please remember that the use of a professional tool will give you a far more accurate result.

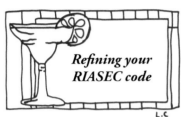

Refining your RIASEC code

The next step is to see if we can get closer to your actual code.

To build on the last exercise however, there now follows a version of an exercise devised by Richard Bolles in his 'What Color is your Parachute' book which will give you more of an insight.

The idea is that ...... *You have been invited to a party!*

Invited to a party!

It is a special type of party, as it is made up of people with each of the different RIASEC codes.

They have been separated into six rooms within the house.

All of the Artistic people are in one room and all of the Entrepreneurial people are in another and so on.

As you arrive and walk up the drive you can hear the noise of the party (although some rooms are much quieter than others).

Enjoy the party - see you there!

As you look around you cannot see anybody you know, so you head to the kitchen, pick up a glass of something to drink and a plate of food and wonder which of the six rooms you will enter.

On the next page, you will find the descriptions of the people in the six rooms.

Joining the party!

Your task, is to choose your first room, from these descriptions and enter the details opposite (e.g. R, Realistic for the first room).

Code e.g. 'R'		RIASEC Area (in words) e.g. Realistic
First room		
Second room		
Third room		

Collecting your thoughts from the party.

20 minutes later, you move to another room. 30 minutes after that, you choose a third (entering the details onto the table again).

Having completed this and left the party please revisit your code at the top of page 113, and in the light of this, make any changes to it, deciding on your final code and enter it below.

My final RIASEC code =

1st	2nd	3rd

Your 'combined' RIASEC result.

Which in words is .....

(please now transfer the code to page 206 within the 'my top 10 interest areas' table at the bottom)

Moving between rooms.

Time to go find the first group of people.. ⟹

THE SIX ROOMS AT THE PARTY.

At the party, room 1 contains 'realistic' (R) people who have mechanical or physical abilities. They enjoy operating equipment or machinery, using tools, and working outside. They tend to follow tradition, have common sense, and take a practical approach to life.

Room 2 contains 'artistic' (A) people who have an appreciation for art, creativity/innovation and self-expression. They may enjoy various types of work related to fine arts, visual arts, foreign languages, writing and other things that utilize imagination. They tend to prefer a more independent and unstructured approach to life.

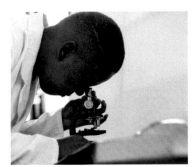

Room 3 contains 'investigative' (I) people who love to learn, analyse, solve problems or conduct research. They are often into subjects related to science, maths, and medicine. They tend to be pretty independent and are often curious about many different things.

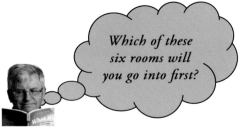

Which of these six rooms will you go into first?

Room 4 contains 'social' (S) people who love working with people in a helping, teaching or training capacity. They enjoy working in team-orientated situations, tend to be very good listeners, and possess good written and verbal communication skills.

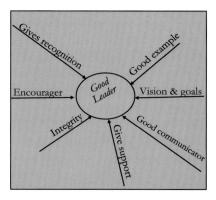

Room 5 contains 'entrepreneurial' (E) people who love to lead, influence, persuade or motivate others. They tend to enjoy power and status, thrive on taking risks and making decisions, and take a spontaneous approach to things. They tend to have good verbal ability. They enjoy meeting new people and the limelight of speaking in public.

Room 6 contains 'conventional' (C) people who love organisation, accuracy and efficiency. They tend to work well with data, numbers, finances, or processes and procedures. They have good follow-through and tend to be structured and methodical in their approach to anything they do.

And which will be next?

119

HOW TO FIND OUT MORE ABOUT YOUR RIASEC CODE

O*NET is a really good online tool for use with the RIASEC model. It can be found at:

https://www.onetonline.org/

Within this resource you will find a link to a useful free RIASEC tool to produce your code:

A good RIASEC research tool to help you find out more

https://www.mynextmove.org/explore/ip

As well as a chance to further research your RIASEC code, the site can also be used to enter your code directly to point to a variety of career ideas.

Use the profiler to give another view of your code.

Having found one that interests you, it is then possible to click on it and find detailed information about the career in which you are interested.

Please ensure you have your **RIASEC** code (from page 117 or the link above) and then continue.

(If you are drawn to any ideas from your RIASEC investigation please note them at the bottom of page 206 exercise seven).

If you need help, please find, starting on the next page, a series of screenshots which show you how to use the RIASEC tool.

Using O*NET to find RIASEC career information

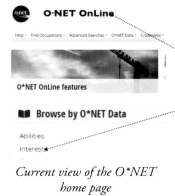

O*NET OnLine features

Browse by O*NET Data

Abilities

Interests

*Current view of the O*NET home page*

Start with finding O*NET by entering on a suitable browser:

https:// www.onetonline.org/

To cross-reference your RIASEC code to career types from the home screen, scroll down and find the interests tab. Clicking on this will take you to a screen which displays an overview of the six RIASEC types.

From here, by clicking on any of the six types, for instance 'realistic', you are taken to a screen where you can enter your own code.

In this example after clicking on 'realistic' you will be presented with a screen which contains the screenshot below - (note it is preloaded with Realistic (R)).

Drilling down further.

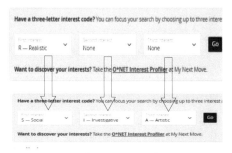

Applying your code.

From this point, you can overlay the boxes with your own code (using the dropdown menus).

In the example opposite I have overwritten the code with SIA.

When you select 'GO', your screen will be updated to show a list of details of careers against your RIASEC code which might suit you.

You can see above, a part of the list of suggested careers for SIA which is also expanded on the right.

If you then click on one of the occupations, it expands into a report for the area (shown below).

Expanded view of above.

A more complete example can be found on pages 124 to 125 which shows a partial report for a 'History Teachers'.

Looking at this you can see the breadth and depth of information available to help you should you choose to use ONET in your career research.

Detailed report.

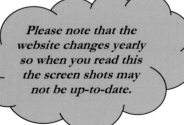

Please note that the website changes yearly so when you read this the screen shots may not be up-to-date.

*The O*NET occupation reports give food for thought.*

O*NET OnLine

Help ▾   Find Occupations ▾   Advanced Searches ▾   O*NET Data ▾   Crosswalks ▾

Occupation keyword search

electrician   Go

Share ▾   Sites ▾

History Teachers, Postsecondary
25-1125.00

🗓 Updated 2022

Teach courses in human history and historiography. Includes both teachers primarily engaged in teaching and those who do a combination of teaching and research.

Sample of reported job titles: Adjunct History Instruction, Adjunct History Instructor, Assistant Professor, Associate Professor, History Instructor, History Professor, History Teacher, Instructor, Lecturer, Professor

Summary   Details   Custom   📖 Easy Read   👤 Veterans   🏴 Español

■ Contents ▾

Occupation-Specific Information

Tasks

▾ 5 of 25 displayed

- Prepare course materials such as syllabi, homework assignments, and handouts.
- Prepare and deliver lectures to undergraduate or graduate students on topics such as ancient history, postwar civilizations, and the history of third-world countries.
- Initiate, facilitate, and moderate classroom discussions.
- Keep abreast of developments in the field by reading current literature, talking with colleagues, and participating in professional conferences.
- Conduct research in a particular field of knowledge and publish findings in professional journals, books, or electronic media.

Technology Skills

▾ 5 of 14 displayed

- **Computer based training software** — Blackboard Learn; Learning management system LMS; Moodle; Sakai CLE
- **Electronic mail software** — Email software: Microsoft Outlook 🔷

 Where ever you see a + you can click on it to get more information

- Word processing software — Collaborative editing software: Google Docs ▲ Microsoft Word ▲

▲ Hot Technologies are requirements frequently included in employer job postings.

Occupational Requirements

Work Activities

> 5 of 21 displayed

- **Identifying Objects, Actions, and Events** — Identifying information by categorizing, estimating, recognizing differences or similarities, and detecting changes in circumstances or events.
- **Getting Information** — Observing, receiving, and otherwise obtaining information from all relevant sources.
- **Updating and Using Relevant Knowledge** — Keeping up-to-date technically and applying new knowledge to your job.
- **Analyzing Data or Information** — Identifying the underlying principles, reasons, or facts of information by breaking down information or data into separate parts.
- **Training and Teaching Others** — Identifying the educational needs of others, developing formal educational or training programs or classes, and teaching or instructing others.

Detailed Work Activities

> 5 of 29 displayed

- Develop instructional materials.
- Guide class discussions.
- Teach humanities courses at the college level.
- Attend training sessions or professional meetings to develop or maintain professional knowledge.
- Stay informed about current developments in field of specialization.

Work Context

> 3 of 19 displayed

- **Freedom to Make Decisions** — 54% responded "A lot of freedom."
- **Structured versus Unstructured Work** — 36% responded "A lot of freedom."

Before you decide on a career, check out if there is a future in it.

O*NET has a lot more to offer you and is worth exploring generally.

Part of the current O*NET 'Find Occupations' screen is shown below.

Note, in particular, the 'Bright Outlook' section. This is where you can find out if a career in which you are interested is expanding (more jobs becoming available) or in decline (jobs decreasing). This will give you an idea on how easy it will be to enter that career.

This information is useful if you are thinking about changing your career (more about this in book five of this series.)

You will also find that some of the jobs are classified as having a bright outlook. On some of the lists you will see a small sun by them. An example is shown below (which we saw earlier).

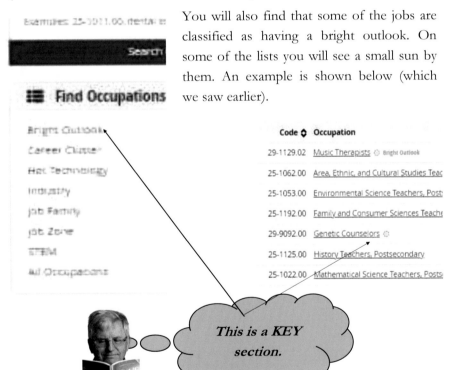

This is a KEY section.

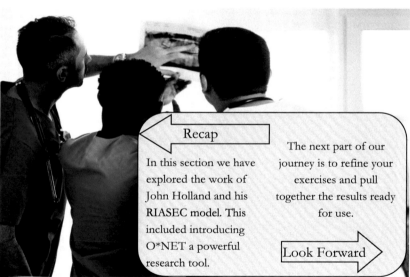

Recap

In this section we have explored the work of John Holland and his RIASEC model. This included introducing O*NET a powerful research tool.

The next part of our journey is to refine your exercises and pull together the results ready for use.

Look Forward

*O*NET can help you find out information about different occupations to help you narrow down your choice.*

We now have something to work with.

STEP 7: PULLING EVERYTHING TOGETHER

Well done for completing the exercises in this book to this point.

This work will lay a solid foundation for your career choices.

Your task now is to combine the interests you have discovered onto a single reference page for use later.

Your interests are one of the key foundation stones for your career.

Interest Area (up to 25)	Priority Review dates			
Priority columns 3,4 and 5 allow you to re-prioritise at a later date against the initial date, column 2)	10 aug 18	12 jan 2019	24 feb 2021	12 sept 2022
Electronics	1	1	2	1
Psychology	2	4	1	2
Counselling	3	2	4	3
Cooking	4	3	3	4
	5			
	6			
	7			

Combining the overall results.

For the initial 25 items you first produced on page 103 (example here), please can you revisit them, re-order if necessary, and then transfer the top ten to the table on page 206.

If the process of doing this causes you to think of a few more, please prioritise and add to the table (ensuring you end up with no more than ten).

Having completed the table, the next step is to add your RIASEC code (from page 117), onto the appropriate space, on page 206 if you haven't already done so.

A reminder, if in exploring your RIASEC code, you have generated some career ideas, there is space for these to be added on the bottom of page 206 (example here).

My RIASEC Code = SAE	In words .... Social, Artistic, \ Entrepreneurial	
Career Ideas suggested by my RIASEC code	Teacher Author	Actor

SUMMARY

Let's pause for another summary. In the last section we have:

- Arrived at a list of your top 10 interests and ...
- Produced your RIASEC code and put them in one place.

At this point, we split into two paths. Firstly, using the information to find a new career and secondly, what to do if you can't.

YOUR CURRENT POSITION ON THE JUNGLE MAP

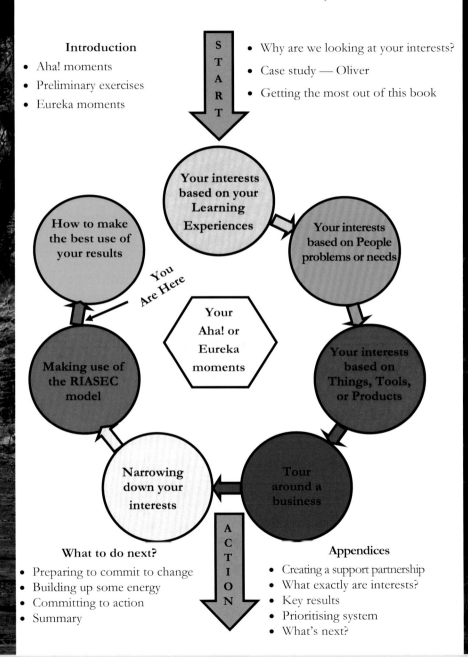

Introduction

- Aha! moments
- Preliminary exercises
- Eureka moments

START

- Why are we looking at your interests?
- Case study — Oliver
- Getting the most out of this book

Your interests based on your Learning Experiences

How to make the best use of your results

Your interests based on People problems or needs

You Are Here

Your Aha! or Eureka moments

Making use of the RIASEC model

Your interests based on Things, Tools, or Products

Narrowing down your interests

Tour around a business

What to do next?

- Preparing to commit to change
- Building up some energy
- Committing to action
- Summary

ACTION

Appendices

- Creating a support partnership
- What exactly are interests?
- Key results
- Prioritising system
- What's next?

HOW TO MAKE THE BEST USE OF YOUR RESULTS

Having a good knowledge of your interests is one of the key parts of your career jigsaw puzzle.

Working with the other books in the series (skills-book two, values-book three and personality-book four), will help you to complete the jigsaw. However, having a knowledge of your interests alone is still useful to you if you find that you cannot access the other books for whatever reason (or you simply decide not to).

A key part of your Jigsaw Puzzle.

On the following pages are the techniques my clients have found of most use.

So, how can a knowledge of your interests alone help?

There are three main ways.

1. Eureka moments

Firstly, just like Kevin on page 12, you may have come across an idea from reading the book and carrying out the exercises which has turned into a solid career idea straight away and you want to explore it further.

For example, you may have noticed the picture of a teacher from the exercise on people and have decided that teaching is the path for you.

Maybe you want to be a teacher?

Alternatively, you may have found an ideal career from looking at the step three exercise 'things' on page 61, or whilst walking round the business in step four page 87.

Or work with money?

If this is the case, then the next step for you is to turn to the Eureka page, page 145.

Or within marketing?

2. Understanding the source of your dissatisfaction

Secondly, a knowledge of your interests will help you to understand your current work situation a little better.

If you find you are unhappy with your career and are not working in, or associated with, your interest area(s) then you may be tempted to incorrectly blame your dissatisfaction on, say, the skills you are using within the interest area, or your personal fit with the people around you.

How can you use the results if you are dissatisfied with your career?

Make sure you know where the problem is.

The issue may, however, be that you are just not interested in the work area(s) themselves. This is the real reason why you are not motivated. The important thing is not to change your skills or the people you work for, without first checking the match to your interests.

You might be better off staying exactly where you are, and changing the job you are doing but using the same skills, for the same employer.

This can be the basis for a useful conversation with your line manager.

Talk it through.

Bathwater — Baby

"Don't throw the baby out with the bath water".

Maybe ask to be reassigned to a different project area in which you are far more interested, without actually changing your company itself.

The key here is not to let a few unsatisfactory areas of your current career determine a complete shift when a change of job within the organisation might solve the problem by itself (I fell into this trap earlier within my own career).

3. Other causes of Mismatch

Thirdly your dissatisfaction may stem from more than just your interest mismatch. If this is the case, how can knowledge of your interests help move you forward and change your career direction completely?

Sometimes you do have to change career completely.

For a career change to be truly successful, knowledge of your skills, values and personality would be beneficial.

However, if you haven't got access to these (or feel a knowledge of your interests on its own is enough) read on for some ideas to help.

CHANGING YOUR CAREER JUST FROM A KNOWLEDGE OF YOUR INTERESTS.

How can you use the information solely on your interests to change your career completely if you haven't had a 'Eureka Moment'? Here are some steps based on the work so far.

Firstly, start with your RIASEC code and use it to guide you to the overall interest area.

Reminder, your code is made up of one, two or three letters from the following six:

- **Realistic (R)**
- **Investigative (I)**
- **Artistic (A)**
- **Social (S)**
- **Entrepreneurial (E)**
- **Conventional (C)**

Start by looking at your RIASEC code.

When you have decided on your code, say SIA, and you are working with a career consultant, you will have been given some resources that cross-reference it to career ideas for consideration (for example see page 115).

I have helped many people by helping them use the RIASEC tool to find new careers.

You may have already added a few career ideas to page 206. If not, and you are working alone with this book, then the following Google search should bring some very useful results.

Search for   -   RIASEC code xxx

for example -   RIASEC code SIA

As an example, the Google search above on 'RIASEC code SIA' produced within the results:

SIA - Chronicle Career Library by Holland Code

Which when clicked on expanded to ⟶

Acute Care Nurses

Clinical Psychologists

Counseling Psychologis

Critical Care Nurses

Health Psychologists

Neuropsychologists

Psychiatric Nurses

Registered Nurses (tem

Registered Professional

Rehabilitation Psycholo

Staff Nurses (registered

Using a Google search on a RIASEC code.

Occupations

Clinical Psychologists
Counseling Psychologists
Developmental Psychologists
Educational Psychologists
Engineering Psychologists
Experimental Psychologists
Health Psychologists
Industrial-Organizational Psychologists
Neuropsychologists
Psychometricians
Quantitative Psychologists

Narrow down.

Clicking on 'Health Psychologists', from above, it further expanded to the occupations list opposite.

This is one example of the resources that you can easily find on the internet. (We have already looked at O*NET earlier in depth on page 120.)

To continue the example above…

Having looked at the above list, you might have decided that you want to look further into the field of Educational Psychology.

The RIASEC model has possibly helped you to identify the actual career (Educational Psychology in this example), however, not necessarily the job within it so we still have some more drilling down to do.

This is where the rest of this book helps in two ways.

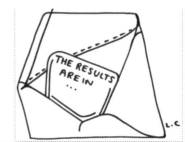

Firstly, referring to your top ten list on page 206 you might have identified that 'Health Services' and 'working with children' are key.

Putting them together we see that you might want to work as an Educational Psychologist in the Health sector - say a job in Child Psychology.

Secondly, the set of preliminary exercises we first met on page Nine also have a role to play which we will move to next.

My Top 10 Interest Areas	
1	*Health services*
2	*Learning*
3	*Travelling*
4	*Working with children*
5	*Psychology*
6	*Talking to people*
7	*Training*
8	*Languages*
9	*First aid*
10	*Computing*
My RIASEC Code =	In words .....

Bring in the Top 10 interest areas.

We have used some of these to help generate your interests. However, they have another important role to play, as we shall see on the next page.

Find a potential career.

WHERE DO THE PRELIMINARY EXERCISES FIT IT?

In exercise six page 202 you identified 'what you wanted more and/or less' of in a career.

This could lie far outside your key interests. For example, the relationship with your line manager, the amount of money you will earn, and your working conditions.

Fitting in the last piece.

The last step in generating your career ideas is to consider how you want to modify them with this information.

These areas are explored in much more depth in books two - 'Skills', three - 'Values' and four - 'Personality'.

Nevertheless, the work we have so far undertaken in the preliminary exercises will serve you well if you decide that the further books are not for you.

Have you done enough?

The following worked examples illustrate how you can use the preliminary exercise to compliment the other work you have carried out.

Let us have a look.

Some examples of generating career ideas follow.

Example One

My RIASEC CODE (p206) = I
(Investigative)

A possible field of work, from
my internet search:

- I (on its own) points to
  "Bicycle Repairers" as an
  option

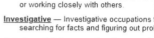

Realistic — Realistic occupations frequentl
    animals, and real-world materials like w
    or working closely with others.

Investigative — Investigative occupations
    searching for facts and figuring out prol

Artistic — Artistic occupations frequently in
    without following a clear set of rules.

Social — Social occupations frequently inv
    service to others.

Enterprising — Enterprising occupations fr
    many decisions. Sometimes they requi

Conventional — Conventional occupations
    details more than with ideas. Usually th

My key Interests (p206)
Point to:

- Security

Selecting/Combining the above
ideas to give:

- Possibly working for a
  supplier of top end bikes who
  specialise in security coding
  and other mechanisms -
  possibly involved with
  designing them.

Whilst ensuring there is more
(p202)...

- Interaction with people

And less (p202)...

- Autocratic management

Make your
own Rainbow

> Note from this example
> that you do not have to
> have all three RIASEC
> letters to make use of
> the tools.

Example Two

My RIASEC CODE (p206) = ISE
(Investigative / Social / Enterprising)

A possible field of work, from my internet search:

- Dietician

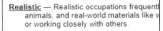

Realistic — Realistic occupations frequentl
animals, and real-world materials like v
or working closely with others

Investigative — Investigative occupations
searching for facts and figuring out prol

Artistic — Artistic occupations frequently ir
without following a clear set of rules

Social — Social occupations frequently inv
service to others

Enterprising — Enterprising occupations fr
many decisions Sometimes they requi

Conventional — Conventional occupations
details more than with ideas Usually th

My key Interests (p206)
Point to:

- Research

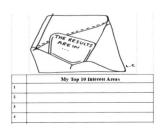

My Top 10 Interest Areas		
1		
2		
3		
4		

Selecting/Combining the above ideas to give:

- Research into nutrition and diets following a higher degree.

Whilst ensuring there is more (p202)...

- Autonomy
- Especially time to think

And less (p202)...

- Nothing comes to mind

Make your own Rainbow

Note that it will also be worth putting the letters in different orders e.g. SIE or ESI and that you might combine this with more than one key interest (in the example above Research and Health).

Example Three

My RIASEC CODE (p206) = CRE
(Conventional / Realistic / Social)

A possible field of work, from my internet search:
- Library Assistant

Realistic — Realistic occupations frequentl
animals, and real-world materials like w
or working closely with others

Investigative — Investigative occupations
searching for facts and figuring out pro

Artistic — Artistic occupations frequently in
without following a clear set of rules

Social — Social occupations frequently inv
service to others

Enterprising — Enterprising occupations fr
many decisions. Sometimes they requi

Conventional — Conventional occupations
details more than with ideas. Usually th

My key Interests (p206)
Point to:
- Business

My Top 10 Interest Areas

1	
2	
3	
4	

Selecting/Combining the above ideas to give:
- Research assistant in the business section of a university reference library

Whilst ensuring there is more (p202)...
- Interaction with people
- Better earnings

And less (p202)...
- Administration

Make your own Rainbow

Ok, your turn next. Please turn to page 207. When you have finished return here.

If you have a career idea, turn the page to see what to do next, or if not please go to page 149 if you do not.

The 'Eureka'
Moment which changes your life

Life changing moment.

WHAT TO DO WHEN YOU HAVE DECIDED ON YOUR NEXT CAREER MOVE AND THE EUREKA MOMENT LANDING PAGE.

The next few pages serve a dual purpose.

This first page is the natural place to be at if you have been working through the book and decided on a potential career, and it also acts as the Eureka landing page (see page 11).

You have decided on a career and want to jump into it.

Maybe you want to get extra input before your make your first move.

Whichever way you arrived here, you have a career related idea to explore further.

The other books in the Inspire career library can help you to refine your career idea, particularly, "the concise guide".

Ideas of how they can help are described In appendix five page 223 'what's next'.

Or maybe you want to get "stuck in" straight away.

Some readers may already be eager to start with what they have gained from this book on its own.

If this is you, where do you start?

The next few pages help.

Taking action when you know where you want to go.

IF YOU ARE HAPPY WITH YOUR CHOICE AND DO NOT WANT ANY FURTHER INPUT, WHAT NOW?

If you're here you probably have a career choice in mind. I would urge you to pause though before you dive in and do some more research.

There are three steps suggested as a minimum.

Firstly, read around the career idea (an internet search on the idea would be a good place to start) and make a list of the questions you would like to research further.

Deciding on the action to take.

Confirm your choice by talking to a few people who have that career (pay for their time if necessary) and ask them the following:

Ask some people who are actually in the career right now.

- The questions you gathered from your background reading.
- What do they like about the career?
- What do they not like about it?
- How did they get into it?
- Do they think there is a future in the career or not?
- How to join if you do not have the entry qualifications?

Secondly, before you commit to the career, *really confirm* that there are job openings for you (for example by using O*NET pages 120 to 127) as well as by asking other people within your network) who may well know.

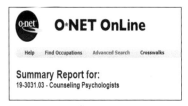

Use online resources.

If you have arrived here after being directed from page 11, but are not ready to commit to a career yet, please return back there now. Otherwise, please turn to page 155 to help you prepare to make a start.

Maybe you are still undecided?

WHAT TO DO IF YOU HAVE GOT TO THIS POINT AND HAVE NOT YET DECIDED ON A CAREER

What to do now?

The Inspire career library is based on a range of books all aimed at helping you move forward within your career in different ways. Within this book we have been on a journey to find the first piece of your career jigsaw puzzle: your interests.

Some land in a different part of this book .

You might have found that this single piece of the puzzle is all you need and you will have ended up at a earlier part of this book to decide what to do next (page 145).

Alternatively, in your particular situation, you might have found that identifying your interests is not enough on its own for your particular situation.

If you are one of the latter, the other parts of the career jigsaw puzzle come into play to help (see page 224).

These will add to the information you now have to allow you to create more career ideas. If neither of these actions describes you, it may be that you have a career blockage preventing you from moving forwards.

Perhaps a bad experience at some point in your career has affected your confidence and self-image.

If this is you, the "concise guide" explores some ways forward (page 228). In particular, it looks at one to one counselling and coaching as possible ways to help (I have helped many clients in this situation). In addition "50 tips to getting unstuck " takes a much deeper dive to help (page 230).

Lastly, some people may not actually want a career at all (and may not even realise it, or may have been 'conditioned' to believe that they do). You may have realised that this is you as you read this.

I Agree ☐

This can easily happen, for example, if you have well-meaning supporters, or parents, keen to see you achieve and encouraging you to 'sign up' to their dream (but not yours).

Maybe you have realised that you do not actually want a career? Maybe you have been conditioned to think that you should have one?

Maybe, for you, a job is a way to make money

If this is you, it can be really hard to feel that you 'should' be doing more (or something completely different).

It is perfectly okay to simply use your working life as a means to finance your outside interests.

You do not have to get any 'higher meaning' out of your career if you do not want to. You can see it solely as a job instead of a career if you want to.

A growing number of people are choosing 'lifestyle careers' where their career is second place to their lives.

For example, 'living in a van' and exploring life whilst working is becoming quite popular. (More on this in book three).

The next story puts it very nicely.

A job can be simply a way to provide resources to finance something else.

THE STORY OF THE FISHERMAN

A young fisherman had just completed his fishing for the day and was sitting and relaxing watching the swans on the water.

Contented.

The management consultant was horrified to find him sat there lazily enjoying the sunset. "Why are you not out fishing he asked?"

Growing

"Because I have caught enough fish for one day" came the reply. "Why don't you catch more than you need" said the management consultant?" "What would I do with them?" came the reply. "You could earn more money and with the cash you could fix a motor to your boat. Then you could go out to where there are more fish and make more money to get bigger nets to fish with."

Soon you would have enough money to buy more boats, create a large fleet and sell the fleet off and make lots more money". "What would I do then?" asked the fisherman." Then you could sit down and enjoy life" said the management consultant.

Worth it?

"What do you think I am doing now?" came the contented reply.

SUMMARY

Let's pause for another summary. In the last section we have:

- Looked at how to use your results to help you make some career based decisions.

On the next stage of our journey, we will encounter a tool that you can use to help you commit to taking action (whether you have a firm career idea or not).

YOUR CURRENT POSITION ON THE JUNGLE MAP

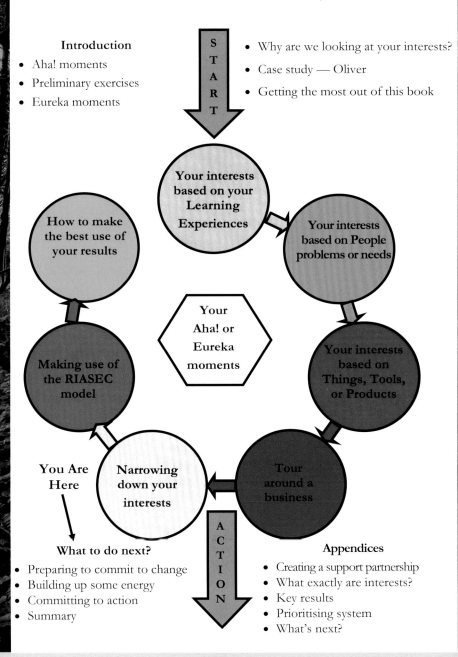

Introduction
- Aha! moments
- Preliminary exercises
- Eureka moments

START

- Why are we looking at your interests?
- Case study — Oliver
- Getting the most out of this book

Your interests based on your Learning Experiences

How to make the best use of your results

Your interests based on People problems or needs

Your Aha! or Eureka moments

Making use of the RIASEC model

Your interests based on Things, Tools, or Products

You Are Here

Narrowing down your interests

Tour around a business

ACTION

What to do next?
- Preparing to commit to change
- Building up some energy
- Committing to action
- Summary

Appendices
- Creating a support partnership
- What exactly are interests?
- Key results
- Prioritising system
- What's next?

What to do next?

Preparing to commit to change - Building up some energy.

In the final exercises numbers 11, 12 and 13 on pages 214 to 216, I am going to ask you to consider committing to some actions.

However, before we do that, some preparation.

Even if you know you want to change, life can sometimes put up barriers. You may have some self-limiting beliefs. For example, you may find you think that some of the following apply (please tick if you do).
I am:

Too old / too young	Size 10 shoe / size 11 shoe (other?)
Over qualified / under qualified	Over weight / under weight
Right handed / left handed	Too introvert / too extravert
Near sighted / far sighted	(space for you to add some)
Too tall / too short	

It takes energy to overcome inertia.

My clients, like you, have taught me that inertia is the real issue. To be honest, they report that it is inertia coupled with a fear of change that saps their will to commit.

It is when clients start to move, and to change, that committing becomes so much easier.

After gathering the initial energy, it is force of will that seems to be the key.

With that in mind, I encourage you to build up two sources of energy to start the ball rolling. This is where we are going next.

On pages 212 and 213 (exercise ten) are two rockets. On the left page, list all the best things that will happen if you do change. On the right page, list the worst things that will happen if you stay where you are.

As you add more and more, feel the energy build, encouraging you to commit. Keep adding. When you are ready, return here. Then let's release the energy and make a start towards moving you forward.

Have you built up enough energy for blast-off?

Are you ready to take some action, make some plans?

COMMITTING TO ACTION

At this point on our journey, you may or may not yet have a definite career idea (if not then, using one of the other books may help, see page 224). Maybe you've decided you want a 'life-style career'. Alternatively, maybe you don't want a career at all!

Time to commit to taking some action.

Whatever position you are in, taking action is the next step. For some, this is easy. For others this is not.

Even if you want to stay exactly as you are, you may need to take some action to make that happen!

What I have learned about myself

Take a while to pause and consider the whole book and complete the following:

Three things I have learned about myself (or possible things I knew and had almost forgotten):

1. *I have an interest in makeup.*
2. *The television and film industry attract me.*
3. *I am fed up with what I am doing now and want to change completely to a different career.*

The following is a simple technique to help. This final series of exercises, starting on page 214 has three parts. An example and instructions follow.

Firstly, consider the whole book and any other thoughts it has brought to mind. Capture up to the top three things that you have learned about yourself connected to your career (see example here).

Please ensure you consider your key aha! moments.

This could include for example, a key interest or a career to move to, or maybe a determination to research some more if you have not yet found a career idea to your liking. Capturing these ideas allows your subconscious mind to work on what you have learnt in the background and put it to good use. Please do that now.

What have you learned about yourself that is helpful?

Welcome Back. Our next step, using page 215, is to consider the top three things you would like to achieve based on the things you have learned about yourself in the last table and capture them. (See below).

Note that you are not being asked to actually commit to any action here. i.e. in the photo opposite the person has released the arrow, taken action.

Hold fire for a moment.

Here, I am asking you to consider where you want to fire the arrow before you release it; to consider what it is you want to achieve, rather than starting to achieve it.

The things I actually want to achieve

Write up to three specific things you want to do in your world of work.

Having done this, rate the probability of you achieving these out of 100.

I want to do the following:

1) Study film and TV makeup professionally and move to a full time career within it

My probability of achieving this out of 100 is 70%

What you want to achieve could range, for example, from deciding on a new career to learning something new to staying where you are (and using the money to buy a campervan and travel!).

Please do that now.

Having decided on some things you want to achieve, how can you improve on your probability of success?

The last stage helps with this.

What do you want to do?

Bring the thoughts together by writing down three things, that you aim to commit to within the next three months (see exercise 13 on page 216 'letter to myself' and the example below).

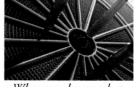

Those three actions should be selected to drive you towards the thing(s) you decided you wanted in the last exercise.

When you know what you want to achieve THEN fire!

The archer fires the arrows and they hit the mark.

My Letter to Myself

Date .....

To be posted to me in three months time on ...../...../......

By the time I receive this letter, I will have started the process of changing my working life towards one which I will love more by completing the following:

(Please be specific, if this is about a new career idea, say what it is and exactly what you will be doing to move towards it).

To help me change career to a make-up artist.

1) *Researched a course at the Ealing Film Studios in London*

2) *Worked with my career counsellor to further match my skills and values against the career*

3) *Made a commitment whether to proceed or look for another career*

KEEPING ON TRACK

How to keep on track especially if on the second step you are showing 'low probabilities' of achieving in some of your areas?

In appendix one, page 17 the idea of working with someone on your journey was introduced.

If you have done this, you will have an ideal support person to encourage you to succeed.

If not, now is the time to share what you are doing with a friend.

Discuss with them the journey you are on and put the 'Letter to myself' in a stamped, addressed envelope and ask your friend to post it to you in three months time. This commitment will encourage you to make it happen.

Recap

In this section we have distilled the learning from the book down into a number of actions to which you need to commit.

As our journey comes to an end the last steps are to present the summary and then the appendices in the next section.

Look Forward

Good luck with the final exercise ... Make it happen!

Two complete examples follow and then it's your turn on page 215, to finish the exercises before returning here.

EX11 What I have learned about myself

Take a while to pause and consider the whole book and then complete the following:

Three things I have learned about myself (or possible things I knew and had almost forgotten):

1) *I really do not want a 'high pressured' career any more.*

2) *I would like to share what I have learnt and encourage the next generation in their goals.*

3) *I am happy to do voluntary work*

EX 12 The things I actually want to achieve

Write <u>up to</u> three specific things you want to do in your own world of work.

Having done this, rate the probability of you achieving these out of 100.

I want to do the following:

1) *Use my Project Management experience and knowledge.*

My probability of achieving this out of 100 is 70.%

2) *Write a book*

My probability of achieving this out of 100 is 80%

3) Become a part-time lecturer.

EX13 My Letter to Myself

Date .....

To be posted to me in three months time on ....../....../......

By the time I receive this letter, I will have done the following things, changing my working life towards one which I will love more:

1) *Used my contacts to explore a possible lecturing position at the local college.*

2) *Produce an outline structure for my own book*

3) *Start a voluntary project management interest group.*

These examples (and the one on the previous page) are from real case studies.

162

EX11 What I have learned about myself

Take a while to pause and consider the whole book and then complete the following:

Three things I have learned about myself (or possible things I knew and had almost forgotten):

1) I have a strong interest in customer service.

2) I would like to be a trainer.

3) Having worked for myself I do not think I could work for someone else again.

EX 12 The things I actually want to achieve

Write <u>up to</u> three specific things you want to do in your own world of work.

Having done this, rate the probability of you achieving these out of 100.

I want to do the following:

1) Develop and present customer service training sessions.

My probability of achieving this out of 100 is 90.%

2) Acquire some consultancy work to enable change of my business.

My probability of achieving this out of 100 is 80%

EX13 My Letter to Myself

Date .....

To be posted to me in three months time on ....../....../......

By the time I receive this letter, I will have done the following things, changing my working life towards one which I will love more:

1) Produce a business plan to consider shutting down my current business and moving into my own training consultancy.

2) Actually present to local group and get feedback.

3) Seek out some customer services training .

Their dreams came true. Books were written, businesses were set up, careers changed.

Approaching the end of our journey in book one.

SUMMARY AND CELEBRATION!

It's time to celebrate your achievements in working through this book!

The achievements to aim for were listed right back at the start on page four As you read through this summary please take the time to reflect on what you've achieved bearing in mind that so many people never even start this journey remaining unhappy in their careers for life.

After following the first six preliminary exercises to capture your current situation, we looked at where your interests originate from (see appendix two, page 177).

Armed with the knowledge that your interests derive from emotions and feelings, we moved onto a further five exercises within the main text. These were then condensed into a key exercise within appendix three, page 206, to draw out your interests and maybe generate a few more.

Please now mark the areas you have achieved on the table on the next page (noting that they won't all necessarily apply to you).

The areas we explored a summary	
Discovering and capturing some aha moments	
Discovering and capturing some Eureka moments	
Finding interests associated with your learning	
Finding interests associated with people problems or their needs	
Finding interests dealing with things, tools or products	
Generating ideas by exploring a fictional company	
Using the RIASEC model in your situation	
Arriving at some career suggestions to consider	
Committing to some action	
Finding a partner to work with	

Possible outcomes from working with the book. Mark the ones that you accomplished in your situation.

My Top 10 Interest Areas	
1	
2	
3	
4	
5	
6	
7	
8	
9	
10	

My RIASEC Code =	In words .....

For many of you, this process will have helped to produce some key information. This could be used to generate a number of career ideas straight away or as a good foundation for further research.

For others, further help may be required and this is discussed at the end of this summary to give you some ideas.

Or maybe, you might have realised that you are, in fact, content with your current world of work and realised that you want to spend more time outside of it, to concentrate on your 'work/life' balance and why not?

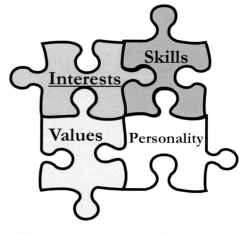

Committing to action.

Wherever your journey through this book has taken you, we will have arrived at the same point— considering the actions you might like to take next. We then ended with a series of exercises to help you structure your next actions and commit to them (exercises 11, 12, 13 pages 214-216).

If you are working with a career consultant, this foundation will provide a valuable insight to build on together.

Working with somebody.

If you are working from these books alone, especially if you find you need more than just an exploration of your interests to determine your next career move, please refer to page 223 to see what is available to answer the question what next?

Or maybe on your own.

Thank you for allowing me to be your guide and I do hope we will meet again in one of the other books within the Inspire career library or maybe in one of my workshops or face to face.

David Carey

David Carey

www.inspirecc.com

davidc@inspirecc.com

01202 605102 from abroad +44 1202 605102

YOUR CURRENT POSITION ON THE JUNGLE MAP

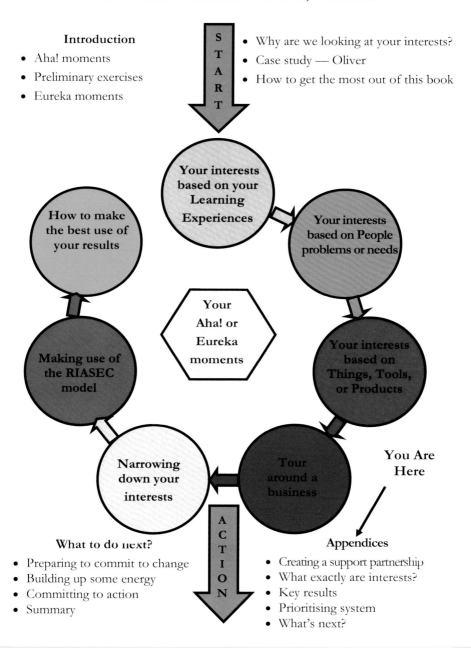

Introduction
- Aha! moments
- Preliminary exercises
- Eureka moments

S T A R T

- Why are we looking at your interests?
- Case study — Oliver
- How to get the most out of this book

Your interests based on your **Learning Experiences**

How to make the best use of your results

Your interests based on People problems or needs

Your
Aha! or
Eureka
moments

Making use of the RIASEC model

Your interests based on **Things, Tools, or Products**

Narrowing down your interests

Tour around a business

You Are Here

A C T I O N

What to do next?
- Preparing to commit to change
- Building up some energy
- Committing to action
- Summary

Appendices
- Creating a support partnership
- What exactly are interests?
- Key results
- Prioritising system
- What's next?

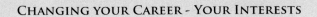

APPENDICES

APPENDIX ONE

CREATING A SUPPORT PARTNERSHIP

Each of the books in the 'Inspire Career Library' will help you to find a key piece of your own career jigsaw puzzle. For some people, working solely with this book will provide the answers they are looking for.

For others, extra input would be useful. Using a career consultant is one way. However there is another.

In appendix one, I would like to invite you to find a partner to work with on your journey.

We will start by exploring one of the key problems finding such a partner will help solve and then move on to discussing how to use such a partnership in practice.

A COMMON PROBLEM

Preparing for our journey.

To help prepare you for your journey through the career jungle, it is useful to start by talking about your habits.

Change often involves swapping bad habits for good ones and/or introducing new ones.

The difficulty is that people start to develop a new habit then slip back into the old one.

This can also very easily happen with career change.

People make some excellent choices. They start to implement them ....

...and it goes wrong.

Why?

They slip back into their old habits.

They don't embrace the changes that have started within them.

What is the answer?

It could be that it lies within the people you know, your "network".

Finding partners on the way will help.

Those with support partnerships of one or more people are much less likely to slip back into old habits.

Hold each other accountable.

I would encourage you to consider this, perhaps find one or more people, from those you know, who want to change their futures and work with them.

The key is to understand what each of you wants as your various journeys develop. Having found someone, hold each other accountable for achieving your goals on the way to your dreams.

As you journey, do not let your partners fall by the wayside.

Ask them to do the same for you.

Invite them on our journey through the jungle. You may find they are quite excited to do so!

Communicate regularly and help each other to set small tasks to move towards the larger goals.

Help each other to avoid changing directions.

The right motivation will help as well.

In 'Think and Grow Rich' by Napoleon Hill this is known as a 'Mastermind Group'.

I have been lucky enough to have had such a partnership (meeting weekly) for a number of years to help me to be accountable for the tasks and goals, that I have set myself. This relationship has been responsible, in no small part, for their achievement.

We meet in the 'local drinking establishment' once a week and if one of us has not completed his tasks, he buys the drinks.

It is an excellent motivator!

(This person is Paul Booker who I mentioned in my dedication).

In appendix two we move onto exploring the role that emotions play.

APPENDIX TWO

WHAT EXACTLY ARE INTERESTS? - WHAT SHOULD YOU BE LOOKING OUT FOR?

Understanding the source of your interests will help you to explore and make better use of them.

However, the psychology of what causes you to be interested in something has not been that widely researched.

What exactly does it mean to be interested in something?

An understanding of what makes you bored at work is invaluable in career selection.

The most relevant work, points at our interests being generated by things that we are emotional about and / or have feelings about.

It is useful, therefore, on our journey together, to explore the difference between emotions and feelings before we proceed.

Starting with exploring our emotions.

Emotions tend to be things which are spontaneous and short lived e.g. being surprised, disgusted, joyous, sad, or angry.

The illustration on page 180 (which is expanded on page 181) shows some of the work of Robert Plutchik who suggests that we have four basic 'pairs of emotions' and that you cannot have both parts of a pair at the same time.

Understanding the difference between Emotions.

Positive emotions.

His theory is that it would be hard to have both the emotions of 'Trust' and 'Disgust' at exactly the same time connected with the same thing.

From combinations of these pairs, other emotions can arise e.g. 'Joy' and 'Trust' can lead to Love.

Negative emotions.

To differentiate them, feelings are emotions which have some thinking attached to them e.g. the emotion of surprise linked with some thinking can give rise to the feeling of curiosity. This is the key ... curiosity can then lead to a long term ***interest*** in the subject.

Emotion (surprise)

Thought

Feeling

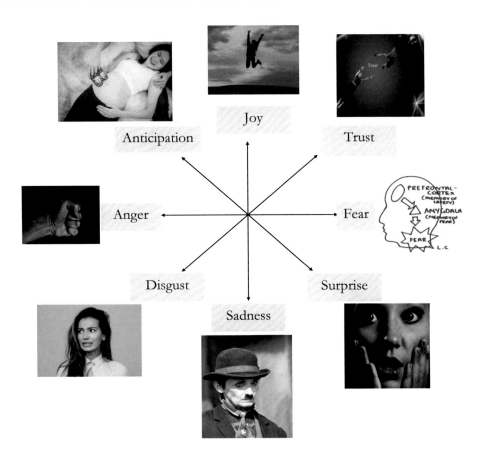

Understanding how the four basic emotion "pairs" of Robert Plutchik (explained on page 179) fit into our journey.

With reference to the expanded diagram on the opposite page you can see the weaker and stronger variants of the basic emotions e.g. a stronger version of fear is terror and a weaker version is apprehension.

Additionally, you can see examples where two emotions combine to produce a third e.g. Serenity and Acceptance = Love.

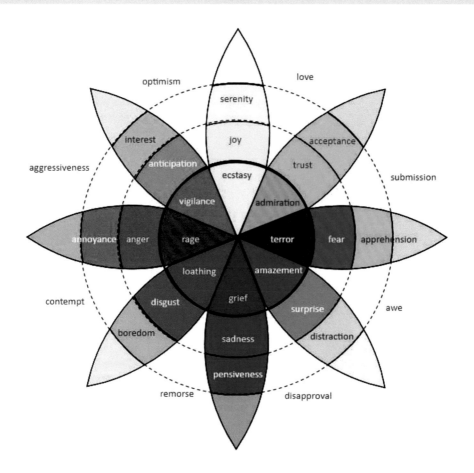

(copied with permission from https://drive.google.com/
filed/1SLwvYy5UgjmvoGnldsbobl06ruo0BNpM/view)

Note that interests itself is also considered as an emotion on Plutchik's wheel. As it is being shown as an emotion this implies that it is considered as being short lived.

It is linking one of the other emotions with curiosity which leads to longer term interests as we shall explore on the next page.

The following examples show the birth of two different long-term interests leading to two totally different careers. Notice that the first interest was born out of a pleasant reaction e.g. that of seeing some amazing graphics in a film (imagine Star Wars or a Disney cartoon).

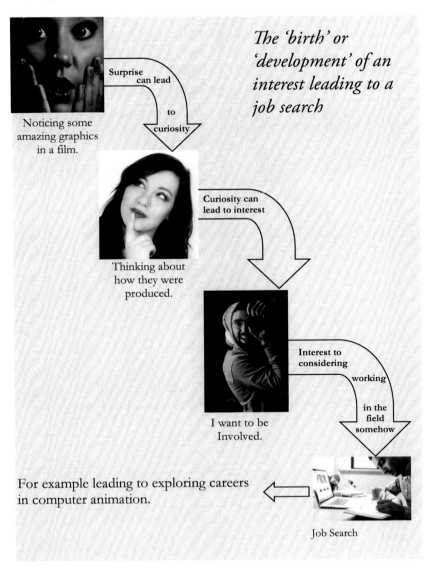

Surprise can lead to curiosity

Noticing some amazing graphics in a film.

The 'birth' or 'development' of an interest leading to a job search

Curiosity can lead to interest

Thinking about how they were produced.

Interest to considering working in the field somehow

I want to be Involved.

For example leading to exploring careers in computer animation.

Job Search

Whereas the second interest was born out of a more unpleasant reaction (e.g. realising people are dying for lack of clean water). The path is,

Surprise ——→ Curiosity ——→ Interest.

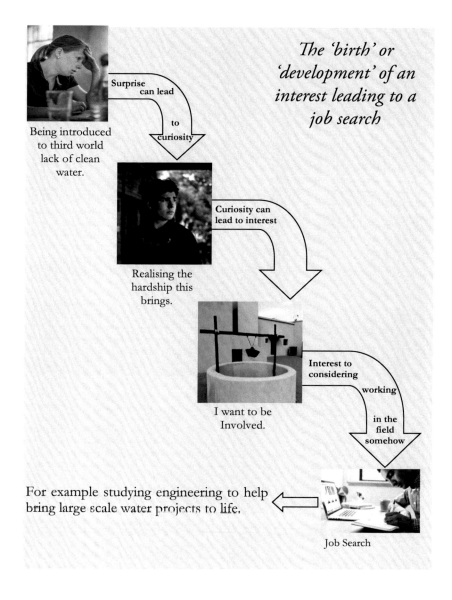

The 'birth' or 'development' of an interest leading to a job search

Surprise can lead to curiosity

Being introduced to third world lack of clean water.

Curiosity can lead to interest

Realising the hardship this brings.

I want to be Involved.

Interest to considering working in the field somehow

For example studying engineering to help bring large scale water projects to life.

Job Search

What emotion or feeling does this picture evoke in you?

FUTURE

TURNING THEORY INTO PRACTICE

Time now to make use of what we have looked at

Having looked at some of the underpinning theory, we turn to some practical exercises (within the main body of the book) with a better understanding of where your interests have come from.

Please watch out for any emotions and feelings which might arise as you complete the exercises.

As a simple example: Does the picture on the opposite page (of the space shuttle taking off) bring any emotions or feelings to mind?

For some, maybe not at all. For others it may evoke feelings of awe, excitement or anticipation of a good future for humanity. This in turn, may lead to wondering how they could be a part of it.

If the picture gives rise to a positive emotion or feeling, then working within the space sector in any capacity will bring a feeling of pride and add to the happiness experienced.

What are the interest areas that you have?

If you were directed to this appendix from the section entitled, 'Why are we looking at your interests?', please now return to page 14 where I am waiting for you.

Research has shown that if all your key results are brought together in one place, they will be more useful to you in the future, as you will be able to find them more easily. To complete this part of our journey, here they are:

APPENDIX THREE

YOUR KEY RESULTS FROM OUR JOURNEY IN ONE PLACE

Please read this bit!

This area of the book allows you to bring together all of your key results as an easy reference for later use.

The first six exercises explore your current situation and how you got there. The following exercises add new thoughts generated by your efforts in reading this book and ends by offering the opportunity to plan some actions to move yourself forward.

The first time you land here you will be completing the 'Preliminary Exercises' (numbers 1 to 6). Please take your time... your past may well hold the key to your future on its own. Please resist the temptation to rush it - allow your past to speak to you.

If you are still in education, and approaching your first career move, you can still make use of these exercises, I have given you guidance within the individual exercises.

EXERCISE ONE - HOW SATISFIED AM I NOW WITH MY CAREER?

In this first exercise, please look at the wheel below. Each 'spoke' represents an area of 'satisfaction' within your current/last position.

The centre of the wheel, '0' represents zero satisfaction. The outside '10' represents the maximum realistic satisfaction you think you could get. I have completed one below to give you an idea of what we are aiming for. Now it's your turn. Please mark where you are on each spoke as follows:

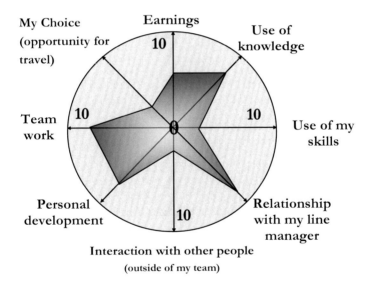

1. To start, pick the top priority areas within your current/last job (this could also be a vacation/temporary job if you have not entered full time employment yet). The following table is there as a guide (please add any categories that are not there which you would like to use).

2. Annotate the wheel with your selection and mark on each axis your score.

3. Join the crosses to complete your wheel as per the example above.

<u>Satisfaction areas</u> — *Remember, this table is just for a start. You could, for example, add a particular skill such as presentation or a value like integrity or a personality trait such as perfectionism.*

Earnings	Relationship with line manager	Team work	Work/life balance
Use of my knowledge	My match to the company culture	Interaction with other people	Autonomy
Use of my skills	Opportunity for self development	Working environment	

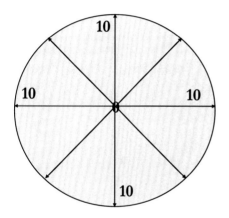

Your invitation to write something whenever you see the pencil.

Take a while to look at your wheel. Identify your key areas of dissatisfaction which if changed would make a big difference. Please make a note of them here with any more detail you wish to add......

Please turn over for preliminary exercise no. two.

EXERCISE TWO - HOW HAVE I GOT TO WHERE I AM NOW?

Having looked at your general satisfaction with your current (or last) position, please review the major steps in your career really thinking about how you have got to where you are today.

If you have not yet started you first career position, please include any voluntary, vacation or part-time work. An example follows.

First job or major change after leaving school. This could also be a move into college or voluntary/temporary or part-time work.	What made you choose this?
I was a field engineer working for a company fixing machines in a territory of banks.	*It was after I failed my A-levels so it was a hard time for me. I wanted a job which was close to electronics but also something easy so I could retake an A-level in the evening and go to college.* *It was all part of a plan just to move to college.*
Looking back how do you feel about the change? What was *good* about it?	Looking back how do you feel about the change? What was *bad* about it?
It showed me that I wasn't good at mechanical things (I had to repair mechanical machines as well as working on electronic ones). *I did develop the ability to work with the public, which later developed into my skill with people.*	*I really wanted to go to university at that point, and found myself in a job instead. I gave it my best though.* *The worst part was working with some of the people there, I just didn't get on.* *I think it was because they knew I wanted to go to college and they resented the knowledge I had which they didn't have.*

Please use extra paper if you need to complete the exercise.

Note that we include any further education. In each case we are looking at the reason for the change and how you felt about it.

Your go now.

By carefully considering the good and bad parts of your career to date, you can really influence the future in your favour.

First job or major change after leaving school. This could also be a move into college or voluntary/temporary or part-time work.	What made you choose this?
Looking back how do you feel about the change? What was *good* about it?	Looking back how do you feel about the change? What was *bad* about it?

Next job or major change e.g. back to education. Please give a brief role description. (If you are still in your first job please continue if you have more to add).	What caused this change to come about?
Looking back how do you feel about the change? What was *good* about it?	Looking back how do you feel about the change? What was *bad* about it?

Next job or major change e.g. back to education. Please give a brief role description. (If you are still in your first job please continue if you have more to add).	What caused this change to come about?
Looking back how do you feel about the change? What was *good* about it?	Looking back how do you feel about the change? What was *bad* about it?

Next job or major change e.g. back to education. Please give a brief role description. (If you are still in your first job please continue if you have more to add).	What caused this change to come about?
Looking back how do you feel about the change? What was *good* about it?	Looking back how do you feel about the change? What was *bad* about it?

Next job or major change e.g. back to education. Please give a brief role description. (If you are still in your first job please continue if you have more to add).	What caused this change to come about?
Looking back how do you feel about the change? What was *good* about it?	Looking back how do you feel about the change? What was *bad* about it?

Next job or major change e.g. back to education. Please give a brief role description. (If you are still in your first job please continue if you have more to add).	What caused this change to come about?
Looking back how do you feel about the change? What was *good* about it?	Looking back how do you feel about the change? What was *bad* about it?

Next job or major change e.g. back to education. Please give a brief role description. (If you are still in your first job please continue if you have more to add).	What caused this change to come about?
Looking back how do you feel about the change? What was *good* about it?	Looking back how do you feel about the change? What was *bad* about it?

Please turn over for preliminary exercise three.

EXERCISE THREE - WHY DO I WANT TO CHANGE CAREER?

In the first exercise we looked at the areas of satisfaction and relative dissatisfaction in your career to date. In this exercise I want to encourage you to delve deeper and explore exactly why you want to change. These might include a particular skill you want to develop, a value to apply or a personality type/trait to satisfy or align against?

If you are still in education, please describe what you are looking for, as far as you are able to, in your first job.

If change is being forced on you (maybe you have been made redundant?) then please take this opportunity to consider which elements of your current career you would change if you could.

I want to change career because..... or .... In my first job I want .....

Please use extra paper if you need to complete the exercise.

Please now condense the above into a few bullet points. (We will be returning to these later to consider the areas you want more of or less of within your career).

Preliminary exercise four is on the next page.

EXERCISE FOUR - IF ONLY I HAD ...

Sometimes we give up too early on a career idea which we then regret later on.

If this resonates within you, I am specifically addressing it within "the concise guide" book of this series (see page 228).

The exercise below gives you a chance to start to think about it now.

It might be that you have had some bad experiences, or maybe you doubt yourself in some way. If you had a passion for something and find yourself thinking 'if only', please complete the below. My suggestion is to carry this career idea through book one for now so that it still has a chance to be considered later. Do not let it slip away completely.

If you are still in education this might be about a subject you gave up.

If only I had ...	I might have ...	What can I do about it now?
Had more confidence.	Had an engineering career.	• Keep it on my interests list. • Develop as a hobby. • Further study.

Please turn over for preliminary exercise five.

EXERCISE FIVE - CAPTURING CURRENT CAREER IDEAS

Taking the opportunity to consider any thoughts arising from the first four exercises as a starting point, take a few moments to capture any career ideas you may currently have below and what draws you towards these ideas.

Please give this quality time, we will be using these later.

Please use extra paper, or the notes pages at the back of the book, if you need to.

Current Career Ideas

	Career	What draws me to it?
1		
2		
3		
4		

The next table is for any careers you would consider (or have considered) however, feel blocked from.

The blockages could be connected to the 'If only I had' exercise or might be down to resources or some other form of limitation.. Whatever they are I encourage you to describe them below if they have stopped you.

Capturing the blockages may help you see them in a different light and if you are working with a career counsellor the basis of a useful discussion.

Career Ideas With Blockages

Career	Blockage?
1	
2	
3	
4	

The last, of the six preliminary exercises is on the next page. $\Longrightarrow$

EXERCISE SIX - WHAT DO I WANT MORE / LESS OF?

We have now reached one of the most important parts of our journey. We will be returning to this later to combine what you have discovered about yourself now, with the results of the other exercises.

This is your opportunity to let your past influence your future.

Please can you carefully review the last five exercises and pull out anything you would like to see more of, or less of, within your next career move.

This information will complement your interests, enriching your career choices.

It would be easy to rush this. I really would encourage you to take your time.

Looking back over the past five exercises which components do you definitely want in your next career move.

> Things I want in my next career move:

Continued

Looking back over the past five exercises, which components do you definitely not want in your next career move. (Of those that remain, are there some which you would still include however like less of?)

Things I don't want in my next career move:

Things I want less of:

The final part of the preliminary exercises is to complete the summary on the next page before returning to page nine.

SUMMARY OF EXERCISES ONE TO SIX

Please can you now review exercises one to six and capture the key items which have arisen for you so far. These will be the areas which will help result in a fulfilling future life, either by ensuring they are present in your life or ensuring they are reduced or totally absent.

Having listed them below, please then review the list and select your top six items.

The key items which have arisen for me from exercises one to six so far are:

Continued:

The top six items are:

Having now completed the preliminary exercises please return to page nine.

EXERCISE SEVEN - PRODUCING MY TOP TEN INTERESTS

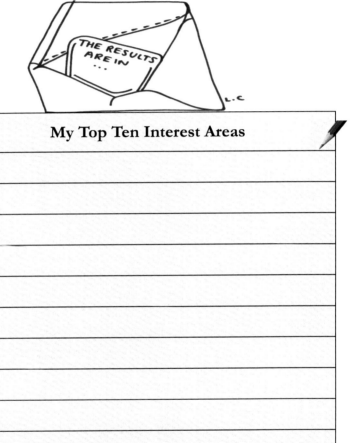

	My Top Ten Interest Areas
1	
2	
3	
4	
5	
6	
7	
8	
9	
10	

My RIASEC Code =	In words	
Career Ideas suggested by my RIASEC code.		

EXERCISE EIGHT - PRODUCING A SOLID CAREER IDEA

It's your turn now to pull the exercises together and see if you can find a career which interests you (I suggest you make a few copies and complete with different variants of your code e.g. SIC, SCI).

My RIASEC CODE (p206) =

A possible field of work, from my internet search:

●

My key Interests (p206)
Point to:

●

Selecting/Combining the above ideas to give:

●

Whilst ensuring there is more (p202)...

●

And less (p202)...

●

Realistic — Realistic occupations frequentl
animals, and real-world materials like w
or working closely with others.

Investigative — Investigative occupations f
searching for facts and figuring out pro

Artistic — Artistic occupations frequently in
without following a clear set of rules.

Social — Social occupations frequently inv
service to others.

Enterprising — Enterprising occupations fr
many decisions. Sometimes they requi

Conventional — Conventional occupations
details more than with ideas. Usually th

THE RESULTS ARE IN ...

My Top 10 Interest Areas	
1	
2	
3	
4	

Make
your own
Rainbow

You might want to make a few copies and put your top choice in here.

EXERCISE NINE—MY 'AHA!' MOMENTS

One of the great things about our journey is that, if you have really taken the time to consider it, you may have had some flashes of inspiration. Suddenly putting things together and thinking aha! this explains why I... (whatever it may be). This is really an intuitive activity and will be easier for some than others. Please use the next few pages to capture your key aha! moments.

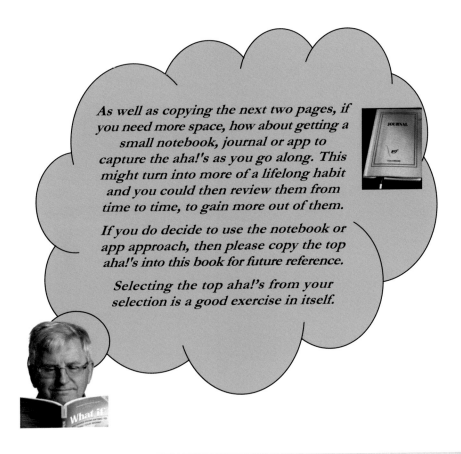

As well as copying the next two pages, if you need more space, how about getting a small notebook, journal or app to capture the aha!'s as you go along. This might turn into more of a lifelong habit and you could then review them from time to time, to gain more out of them.

If you do decide to use the notebook or app approach, then please copy the top aha!'s into this book for future reference.

Selecting the top aha!'s from your selection is a good exercise in itself.

Things I have learnt about myself:

Things I have learnt about myself:

Things I have learnt about myself:

EXERCISE TEN — GIVING YOU AN ENERGY BOOST!

Having completed the last nine exercises, the next port of call is an opportunity to build up enough energy to commit to some action, to help you move forward.

The best that will happen if I change.

The worst that will happen if I do not change.

Now please return to page 156.

EXERCISE 11 — WHAT I HAVE LEARNED ABOUT MYSELF

Take a while to pause and consider the whole book, including the aha!'s, and complete the following:

Three things I have learned about myself (or possible things I knew and had almost forgotten):

1)

2)

3)

EXERCISE 12 — THE THINGS I ACTUALLY WANT TO ACHIEVE

Write <u>up to</u> three specific things you want to do in your world of work.

Having done this, rate the probability of your achieving these out of 100.
I want to do the following:
1)

My probability of achieving this out of 100 is ....

2)

My probability of achieving this out of 100 is ....

3)

My probability of achieving this out of 100 is ....

EXERCISE 13 - MY LETTER TO MYSELF

Date .....

To be posted to me in three months time on   ....../....../......

By the time I receive this letter, I will have changed my life for the better, by doing the following things:

(Please be specific, if this is about a new career idea, say what it is and exactly what you will be doing to move towards it).

1)

2)

3)

Don't forget to commit and post your letter to somebody who will hold you accountable if you really want to see these changes happen.

Appendix Four

Prioritising system

Earlier in the book (on page 100) I presented a you with simple prioritising system for use with sorting your interests.

On the next two pages is a more effective prioritising system if you wish to make use of it.

It does take a lot more time to complete however I do feel it is worth it if you want to go down this route.

This exercise works by picking up each card, one at a time, and deciding its priority against the others tallying your preferences as you go (described in detail below). This is another one of those thought-provoking tasks which would benefit from some real quality time.

PRIORITISING TOOL

Step one: Before you start, you will need a number of cards or post-it notes. Put one of your interests on each and spread them out on a table or surface as per the example below.

Step one, start with all of the cards on the table.

Step two, take a card and keep this in your hand.

Leaving a gap on the table.

Step two: Take any one of the cards as per the example above, (it really doesn't matter which one). Compare it with each of the cards on the table in turn. As you compare the one in your hand to each value on the table tally the one you value the most, the one in your hand or the one on the table by putting a mark on it.

Keep comparing the one in your hand with the rest of the cards on the table adding tally marks until you have compared it against all of them as you can see on the next page.

When completed put the card in your hand aside (you will not be adding any more tally marks to it).

You should now have one completed card put to one side with the rest of the cards left on the table as per picture opposite, some with tally marks and some without.

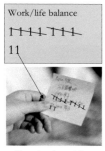

Work/life balance

11

Cards left on the table (with tally marks) which will be as per page 220 minus one card, in this case the card work / life balance.

Completed card from the 1st pass which is now set aside.

Tally marks on the other cards.

Step three: Select another card from the table (again it does not matter which one) and repeat the process. You should now have two cards completed and set aside (see example below work/life balance & autonomy). Repeat the process until you have only one card left on the table.

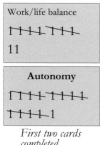

Work/life balance

11

Autonomy

First two cards completed.

Cards left on the table (with tally marks) which will be as per page 220 minus two cards in this case work / life balance and autonomy.

Step four: You can now simply add the last card to the newly created pile of cards with tally marks on (as you will have nothing left to compare it against) and you will have finished.

The card with the most tally marks on will be your top priority and the one with the least your bottom. It is now just a case of selecting the top 25 cards with the most tally marks, put them in front of you, and you are done and are ready to return to page 99.

If you find you have two cards of the same priority, flip a coin to decide which has the higher priority. While the coin is in the air you may have a feeling as to which way you want it to land! If so, go with your feeling! If not let the coin decide!

What's next?

APPENDIX FIVE

WHAT'S NEXT?

Having completed this book I hope you will be wondering what's next? Where do I go from here?

It might be that you now know exactly what you want to do, and have some resources in place to help you to take the next step on your journey. However if you haven't, here are six ideas which might help you (all of which are explained in more depth on the following pages):

- Get hold of another one of the books in the series
- Attend one of the Inspire Career Consultancy workshops
- Have some 1:1 career counselling specifically focused on you
- Get some specific help if you have been made redundant
- Make use of the free material on the Inspire website
- The 'First Friday Free' initiative (page 239)

If you are interested in any of them please contact me to discuss.

For full contact details please see First Friday Free page 239.

A BRIEF PREVIEW OF THE WHOLE SERIES AND OTHER SERVICES

If you have journeyed together with me this far you will have established a key piece of your own career jigsaw puzzle.

Each of the books in the Inspire Career Library adds its own value, its own piece of the puzzle.

Working with all of them however brings more than the sum of the whole.

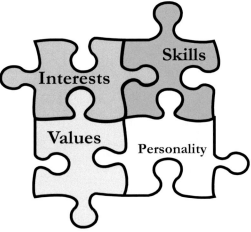

Books one to four explore the pieces of the jigsaw puzzle if you want to go further.

So what is in the other books and how might they help you?

The books are all intended to stand alone, however they have been written in sequence to encourage you to take a deeper dive.

To order any of the books directly from Inspire Career Consultancy, at a discount (and to find out about the release dates, and to view short videos on each book for more detail on how they could help you), please visit:

David Carey

www.inspirecc.com/books

YOUR INTERESTS

THE REST OF YOUR LIFE...

AVERAGE

MEMORABLE

What sort of career do you want?

For many, the Interests book is the first encounter with your career jungle. It is where you accept the invitation to explore it and see what is there.

We start by looking at how you have got to where you are now finding out what you are satisfied with generally and what you are not.

We consider what would have happened 'if only I had ….' (whatever that might be) and if you can do something with that now.

Early on in the journey, you are introduced to 'aha!' and 'Eureka' moments and encouraged to look out, and act on them.

We then move to exploring your interests in depth, both those you know something about and those you have yet to discover. Having achieved this our last port of call is to produce some solid career ideas and explore how to commit to action and make change happen!

The interests book is an excellent introduction to the series as well as a powerful book in its own right.

To view a brief video on the content of this book please refer to the link on page 224.

YOUR SKILLS

Within the skills book, we enter your career jungle and consider your skills and realise how using, or not using these, affects the happiness in your career.

This book will help you to assess how to be happier by identifying and developing the skills you want to use more of and by decreasing the use of those you want to use less of.

Additionally, if you have no idea of what you want to do next then this book will allow you to see where an identification of your skills can help.

Lastly, if you know the career you want to change to, this book will have identified skills which you can use as 'bargaining chips' to help in the interview process. To view a brief video describing more about this book and for the release date please refer to the link on page 224.

The skills I would like to use **MORE OF:**	The skills I would like to use **LESS OF:**
1	1
2	2
3	3

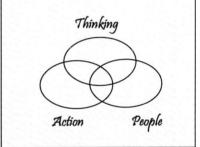

Exploring your three clusters of skills.

Using your skills as bargaining chips.

YOUR VALUES

Within the values book, we explore your values. Values are beliefs that influence your behaviour, attitude and decision making in everyday life.

Our Values Are Our Roadmap For Success

Your values give you an important 'internal compass' to steer your whole life by.

They can help answer questions such as:

- Which career is the best for me?
- Is this promotion a wise choice?
- Would starting my own business work for me?
- Do I compromise, or be firm with my position?
- Does this company fit my values?

To view a brief video describing more about this book and for the release date please refer to the link on page 224.

YOUR PERSONALITY

Within the personality book, we turn our attention to how an understanding of your personality affects your career choices.

The book starts by exploring exactly what personality is and introduces you to two key theories.

The majority of the book is given over to taking you on a personal journey of discovery through your personality collecting 'aha!' moments along the way.

People who have used this book have found it quite transformative and helpful. In particular, it has helped them to understand events that have slowed them down in the past.

To view a brief video describing more about this book and for the release date please refer to the link on page 224.

THE CONCISE GUIDE

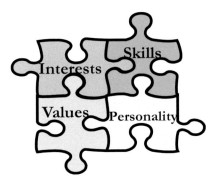

As well as practical guides aimed at helping you generate career ideas, the concise guide is where you have an opportunity to extract all that you have learnt on our journeys within the other four books (if you have used them) and by joining them together, gain even more.

The book is broken down into four distinct parts.

In part one, we start by exploring a number of approaches to help you generate a range of career ideas to add to those you may have already created, either on your own or, by using the other books in the Inspire Library.

Part two moves onto combining all you have learnt from the other books into a whole. It then turns them into a decision making tool which you can apply to the ideas generated in part one. This tool will assist you in making the best choice (There are simplified exercises to follow if you don't have access to the other books to draw on).

In part three, we move onto examining your selected choice in finer detail by looking at any constraints and/or concerns you may have and how to overcome them, or if that is not possible, what to do next.

In part four we turn our attention to the next move, including where to go for extra help. Finally, we bring it all together in our closing thoughts. To view a brief video describing more about this book and for the release date please refer to the link on page 224.

FIND YOUR NEXT JOB IN FIVE STEPS

This book is the ideal companion to any of the initial books in the series. It is focused on helping you to find your next job.

It allows you to take the ideas generated and move into the career you are interested in by:

- Generating a CV
- Maximising Job search techniques
- Preparing for an interview
- Negotiation techniques
- Making a good impression in the first 30 days in your new job.

START YOUR OWN BUSINESS IN 10 STEPS

If you have decided that starting your own business is for you, however you don't know where to start, this is the book for you!

It will help you by:

- Generating a business idea
- Finding a vision, a strategy, and some goals to get there

Producing a marketing plan covering:

- Deciding on the product or service itself
- How to promote it
- Its place in the market
- The price to sell at

Additional considerations:

- Considering the infrastructure
- Finding out how to sell
- Legal considerations
- Looking at the financial side

To view a brief video describing more about these two books and for the release dates please refer to the link on page 224.

These books will help you get off to a good start whichever path you take.

ARE YOU STUCK DECIDING ON YOUR NEXT WORK MOVE! 50 TIPS TO GETTING UNSTUCK !

This book is aimed specifically at those of you who are trying to make a move in the world of work and feel stuck.

Does any of this ring a bell? You:

- Feel under pressure to make a decision

- Just feel totally de-motivated

- Are seeing your friends move forward, happy for them however sat at home just wondering—what should I do next?

- Feel that your confidence is at rock bottom

- Feel like you are "walking through treacle"

- Feel it is easier to stay where you are

- Are afraid about what the future might bring to you

Within this book, we are going to explore the reasons why you might be stuck followed by 50 practical tips to getting you unstuck and into a new life.

I have spent a good amount of time within Inspire Career Consultancy working with people who are stuck and it is always a joy to see them become unstuck and move forward into new futures.

My hope is that this book will do the same for you. To view a brief video describing more about this book and for the release date please refer to the link on page 224.

HAVING A GREAT RETIREMENT
50 TIPS TO A PERFECT RETIREMENT!

You have worked hard and the time has come to explore what life has to offer next.

Maybe you have it all planned out, or maybe you are taking each day as it comes. There isn't a "one size fits all".

Nearly all of the books on retirement focus on money and have just a little on what you are going to do with your time. This book is different!

It is very likely in today's world that you can look forward to 20 to 30 years of retirement. That is much more time than you probably spent in acquiring your education or raising your family and a huge chunk of the time you spent working.

These 20 to 30 plus years bring with them three core questions:

- What are you going to do with the time?
- Are you healthy enough—or can you be?
- Can you afford what you want to do?

In this book, we will be going on a fun journey exploring these questions together. There will be lots of "doodle time" with ideas to ponder over and produce "aha!" moments. I wonder, what will yours be?

We are of the "Back to the Future" generation and as Doc Brown said:

"Your future is whatever you make it—so make it a good one!

I feel that in this decade we have more opportunity than ever to "make it a good one". The 50 tips in this book are there to help.

To view a brief video describing more about this book and for the release date please refer to the link on page 224.

INSPIRE CAREER CHANGE WORKSHOP

How would you like to spend a weekend away from distraction, focusing entirely on your career? How much could that be worth to you?

This is the opportunity being offered here.

You will be part of a select group of like-minded people with one aim in mind; to move you out of your current working situation, which you maybe dislike, or are just not suited to, into one that you will love with a bright, promising future.

The weekend will comprise of a series of exercises to explore, in depth, your interests, skills, values and personality which can be used on their own or in conjunction with the books in this series.

After each exercise, you will break into pairs and help each other explore the results of the exercises to take a deeper dive and gain even more value.

As the weekend progresses you will build up a more, and more, detailed picture of what you are looking for in your ideal working life.

You will also have an additional bonus, that of understanding how to get more out of the rest of your life as well.

At the end of the weekend you will have a valuable opportunity.

This is to transfer the key data from the exercises onto a flipchart sheet and present it to your assembled group of peers (I will be one of those).

WHY IS THIS SO VALUABLE?

By this time you will have worked together, in differing pairs, and will know each other quite well. I will have selected people for the group to ensure that at this point you will all have each other's interests in mind, looking to help.

All of you will be experienced people in your own right with quite differing backgrounds and needs.

With all of the valuable, assembled life experiences in the room the potential to make some key observations on your flipchart data will be enormous.

Each person in the group will be given 30 minutes to invite input on a key question of their choice, with the potential for real change in your life.

In previous groups, people have used this opportunity to ask:

- What career do you think I would be suited for most?
- Do you think starting a business would be a good idea for me?
- How can I achieve a better work/life balance and reduce stress levels?
- How do you think I could move into an active retirement from here?

This workshop has the potential to change your working life and beyond. I would value the opportunity to discuss it in more depth and see how it could match your background and needs.

To find out more about the workshop and why it might help you please contact me on 01202 605102 (+44 1202 605102) or see my video at:

www.inspirecc.com/workshop

ONE-TO-ONE CAREER COUNSELLING AND CONSULTANCY

You can change your working situation at any time in your life. So many people are in careers they hate. Don't let this be you.

If you truly want to move from a working life that you dislike, into one that you love then having one-to-one attention, specifically on you, might be the 'Rolls-Royce' standard.

Inspire offers you just that. A tailored service specific to your own situation, whether you are having career issues, challenges in starting your own business or problems running it.

These sessions can be conducted at our offices, by phone or video conference (for example Zoom, Microsoft Teams etc).

It all starts at the first session where we will explore who you are and your specific issues.

Armed with this information, together, we will produce a set of well formed goals to address your needs. We will then discuss exactly how we can achieve these goals to move you into a new life and make a start.

The sessions come with free copies of my books and, depending on your needs, professional psychometrics. Is the 'Rolls-Royce' option the one for you?

For more information about how I can help you please visit:
www.inspirecc.com/counselling

HELPING WITH REDUNDANCY—IF IT'S AFFECTING YOU PERSONALLY

If you are about to be made redundant, or you have already been, this section is particularly for you. Inspire has helped literally hundreds of people who have been in the unfortunate situation of being made redundant, Although I am not 'in your shoes' it has happened to me twice in my life as well.

So, how can I potentially help you? This is a time when you might need to get a job quickly and need help with things like your CV and interview techniques. Or it might be a time when you want to stand back and have a think about what you want to do with your career now? Maybe you just need somebody to talk with, to help you think through what to do next? It would be a privilege to do just that as someone once did for me.

Whatever your situation, I would welcome the opportunity to get along side you and see if I can help.

Please have a look at the 'First Friday Free' initiative (page 239) to see if this might be a good starting point to help you. Or please just give me a ring, as a few minutes on the phone (no charge) may help you start to move forward and I will try and fit you in as soon as I can.

For more information about how I can help you please visit:
www.inspirecc.com/redundancy

HELPING WITH REDUNDANCY—IF YOU NEED TO LET SOME OF YOUR EMPLOYEES GO

If you are in this situation, you may also be facing a time of management stress within your organisation however, at the same time, still wanting to help the employees you need to say goodbye to.

Inspire offers the opportunity to help your company treat your employees with respect and dignity.

Getting alongside individuals, at a time like this, often requires more time than managers feel they can give. They also feel perhaps unskilled to do this, even though they really want to help.

To have an external person talk to your employees, in complete confidence, is often the thing they need right now.

We call this 'outplacement services'. As well as helping the employees that are leaving, it can have a positive effect on the people remaining within the company so that they know, that if it did happen to them, there will be someone to help (encouraging key people to stay rather than look around).

Inspire has worked with hundreds of people in a variety of settings from one-to-one sessions to career workshops, both in-house, and off-site or simply on the phone or by providing copies of these books to assist.

If you would like to talk about your companies situation I would welcome a call (full contact details on page 239).

For more information about outplacement services please visit:

www.inspirecc.com/outplacement

FREE RESOURCES FROM INSPIRE'S WEBSITE

www.inspirecc.com

It is my intention to add more and more new information, that may help you, to the Inspire website in the form of free video and textual material. As an example, you can gain so much in life by listening to other people's stories. Here is a selection from the success stories tab on the website.

Can listening to their stories help you?

Re-energising a career	Coping with redundancy	Midlife career change	Saving a passion which was almost lost
Helping to consider a next career move	Finding employment later in life	From self-employment back into employment	Helping with the birth of a new business

The difference a good CV can make	Changing a career after two sessions	Helping with early career decisions	Moving away from "the same old same old"
Developing an existing business	From head teacher to electrician	A new career in your 70s	Breaking the cycle of bouncing from one job to another

To see, and hear, these success stories (and others) please scan the QR code below, or enter the following into your browser.

www.inspirecc.com/stories

FIRST FRIDAY FREE

If you have read the rest of the book, you will probably have gathered by now that Inspire is my personal mission in life and it is all about helping you in your working life.

We all need to make an honourable living. However, I truly believe that if we can give a little back in this hectic world that we may all move forward together into a more contented future.

With this in mind, please can I introduce you to 'First Friday Free'.

I will be setting aside the first Friday of each month so that I can be of assistance in any career or business issues you may have.

To make use of 'First Friday Free', please contact me and together we can book a slot for the first available Friday.

Wishing you all the best in your future.

David Carey
davidc@inspirecc.com
www.inspirecc.com/First-Friday-Free
01202 605102
from abroad +44 1202 605102

ONE LAST MESSAGE

Congratulations!

I am really pleased that you made the decision to improve yourself by exploring the strategies, examples and case studies in this book. I admire you for wanting to improve yourself and your life.

My mission within this book was to serve you and make a positive difference in your life by inspiring you to think and act differently.

My hope is that I have done just this and have inspired, and empowered, you to make the moves in life that you deserve.

Whether you achieve your visions and goals is up to you. No one can promise or guarantee that your dreams will come true.

However, by following simple strategies like the ones in this book, I truly believe you can accomplish anything you want to.

And the best time to start it is now!

And once again, congratulations!

"LUCK IS WHERE PREPARATION MEETS OPPORTUNITIES"

Roman philosopher Seneca

ACKNOWLEDGEMENTS– THANK YOU

I couldn't have completed this book without the help of so many of you who have contributed so much by supplying material, giving testimonials, proofreading, inspiring me, encouraging me and showing excellent examples of how to communicate well—thank you. There are so many of you and if I have forgotten to add your name below please accept my sincere apologies.

Alan Roberts, Andy Lee, Andy Whale, Angela Squires, Anne Hedges, Barbara Cox, Barry Faith, Catherine Carey, David Hassall, David Samuel, Deane Kustner, Dee Steed, Eric Carey, Fabian Lochner, Graham Carey, Helen Rogers, James Sale, Jane Kustner, Jasmine Peckham, Jason Davies, Jason Routley, Karen Nelson, Kate English, Kelly Budd, Kevin Potter, Laura Carey, Laura McHarrie, Laurie Clow, Lee Haensel, Lisa Cavany-Barton, Maurice Howell, Megan Unsworth, Nick Unsworth, Oliver Simpson, Pam Carey, Patches Chabala, Paul Booker, Paul Carey, Penny Carey, Pete Elliot, Peter Westwood, PJ, Richard Rider, Rick Ford, Sarah Pix, Sam Bolton, Sandra Stirling, Seun Oladosu, Stephen Feltham, Stuart Dyson, Stuart Wyatt, Susan Carey, Tania Booker, Teresa Allwood, Tessa Rogers, Tessy Ogidi, Tom Parr, Vanda North, Vivian Messiah, Zafer Hussain,

And in memory of my departed close friends: *Brian Masterman, Paul Moss*

There are three people I would like to particularly acknowledge. The first is Richard Bolles of 'What color is your parachute' fame. Richard's book has influenced my whole career and not just this book. I was privileged to meet him once and I have a memory of a very modest gentle man. Secondly, Rob Nathan of Career Consulting Services (CCS) (rob@career-counselling-services.co.uk). Rob gave me some of my own training some 20 years ago and some of my exercises have been influenced by his training. Lastly, Dr Roy Childs of TeamFocus (teamfocus.co.uk). Roy taught me not only the basics of psychometrics and in particular his TDI tool but more importantly how to use the TDI to help people understand themselves and move towards change.

I can recommend CCS for anybody wanting training in career consultancy and TeamFocus for anybody wanting a very good grounding in psychometrics and access to professional tools.

ABOUT DAVID CAREY

MSc., DMS.,PGDip.,CEng.,MIET.,MCMI

David Carey is a Christian who has extensive skills, developed over many years, within the areas of Engineering, Training, Employment Development, Career Counselling and Business Consultancy.

He has gained experience within the both corporate and small business environments spanning the private and voluntary sectors resulting in several local and national training awards.

Organisations which have benefited from David's assistance include:

British Telecom GEC-Marconi

NTL   Virgin Media

Royal Mail   Vodafone

Plessey   YMCA

Thompson   Hope FM radio

David created Inspire Career Consultancy (www.inspirecc.com) in 2002 to help both individuals and companies.

Previous achievements have included the development of an internationally accredited professional career development scheme. This was the first under the, then, new rules for achieving chartered engineering status – SARTOR 97 (Standards And Routes To Registration).

David complements his work with local community involvement, rose to the position of Vice-President Wessex branch of the Chartered Management Institute and has taken an active role in the Prince's Trust, assisting a variety of start-up businesses. He is currently active in the voluntary sector assisting DORMEN (Dorset Mentors) by supporting developing businesses.

A frequent speaker on career-related topics, David's motivation is to inspire the fulfilment of others in their work.

Your Notes

Your Notes

Your Notes